Better Homes and Gardens®

celebrate the SEASON

2000

Better Homes and Gardens® Books
Des Moines, Iowa

Better Homes and Gardens® Books
An imprint of Meredith® Books

Celebrate the Season 2000
Editor: Vicki L. Ingham
Assistant Food Editor: Chuck Smothermon
Contributing Editor: Joyce Trollope
Contributing Writers: Lisa Kingsley, Jil Severson
Art Director / Graphic Designer: Marisa Dirks
Copy Chief: Catherine Hamrick
Copy and Production Editor: Terri Fredrickson
Book Production Managers: Pam Kvitne, Marjorie J. Schenkelberg
Contributing Copy Editor: Diane Doro
Contributing Proofreaders: Judy Friedman, Beth Lastine, Elizabeth Duff-Popplewell
Principal Photographer: Peter Krumhardt
Indexer: Elizabeth T. Parson
Electronic Production Coordinator: Paula Forest
Editorial and Design Assistants: Kaye Chabot, Judy Bailey, Mary Lee Gavin, Karen Schirm
Test Kitchen Director: Lynn Blanchard

Meredith® Books
Editor in Chief: James D. Blume
Design Director: Matt Strelecki
Managing Editor: Gregory H. Kayko
Executive Shelter Editor: Denise L. Caringer

Director, Retail Sales & Marketing: Terry Unsworth
Director, Sales, Special Markets: Rita McMullen
Director, Sales, Premiums: Michael A. Peterson
Director, Sales, Retail: Tom Wierzbicki
Director, Sales & Marketing, Home & Garden Centers: Ray Wolf
Director, Book Marketing: Brad Elmitt
Director, Operations: George A. Susral
Director, Production: Douglas M. Johnston

Vice President, General Manager: Jamie L. Martin

Better Homes and Gardens® **Magazine**
Editor in Chief: Jean LemMon
Executive Interior Design Editor: Sandra S. Soria
Executive Food Editor: Nancy Byal

Meredith Publishing Group
President, Publishing Group: Christopher M. Little
Vice President, Finance & Administration: Max Runciman

Meredith Corporation
Chairman and Chief Executive Officer: William T. Kerr

Chairman of the Executive Committee: E. T. Meredith III

All of us at Better Homes and Gardens® Books are dedicated to providing you with information and ideas to enhance your home. We welcome your comments and suggestions. Write to us at: Better Homes and Gardens Books, Shelter Editorial Department, 1716 Locust St., Des Moines, IA 50309-3023. Visit us at bhg.com. or bhgbooks.com.

If you would like to order additional copies of this book, call 800/439-7159.

Cover photograph: Peter Krumhardt

Our seal assures you that every recipe in *Celebrate the Season* has been tested in the Better Homes and Gardens® Test Kitchen. This means that each recipe is practical and reliable and meets our high standards of taste appeal. We guarantee your satisfaction with this book for as long as you own it.

family

and friends are central to holiday celebrations. In this book, you'll find lots of ideas for focusing on family in fun and creative ways—a centerpiece of paper dolls made from photos, a tablecloth with pockets for snapshots and souvenirs, a game based on your own family's history. Your cultural heritage also can be the starting point for decorations and activities—see pages 46–53 for inspiration. If you already incorporate your family's heritage into your decorations, I'd love to hear about it (write to the address on page 2). In this volume, for example, some of the Hanukkah projects were suggested by a reader in California. Let me know what other kinds of decorating projects and party ideas you'd like to see, too. This year, we're suggesting a wine and cheese party for something simple, or a quiet sit-down dinner for a more formal gathering. Either will bring people together for a festive evening. Being with loved ones makes the season merry.

Vicki Ingham

— Vicki Ingham, Editor

3

table *of* contents

setting the stage

gathering together

5

giving from the heart

kids' stuff

In a Twinkling
Easy-to-use ideas for the holidays

SETTING

If the urge to simplify your life is at odds with your desire to fill your home with a festive spirit, try this: Plan basic decorations, then add or subtract elements to change the holiday personality. Or do the unexpected: Shop your own closets and attic or basement for items with which to create displays. Bring out everything red and white you can find, for example, and arrange it on the mantel. Add a few boughs of fresh greenery and some sparkly ornaments, and you have a display that says "Merry Christmas" in a delightfully fresh and personal way. Using what you have—not just ornaments and holiday items, but favorite collections and everyday objects—makes seasonal decorating creative and fun. Enjoy the process.

the STAGE

7

Dress your home in new clothes for the season with slipcovers, pillows, a hearth rug, and window scarves.

happy holiday *makeover*

The wardrobe shown here is easy to make from painters' canvas drop cloths, using fabric inks and rubber stamps to supply the holiday motifs.

Dress up your everyday pillows with a button-on overlay or a grommeted tie-on slipcover. Then decorate the mantel, and you're set.

before

after

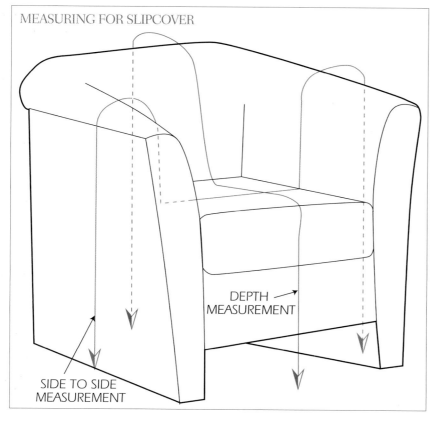

MEASURING FOR SLIPCOVER

DEPTH
MEASUREMENT

SIDE TO SIDE
MEASUREMENT

chair slipcover

here's how...

1 To determine the size for the drop cloth, measure the chair as shown in the diagram. Add 24 inches to the side-to-side width measurement. Add 12 inches to the depth measurement. Cut the canvas to these measurements, piecing it if needed. Hem any raw edges.

2 Using a single large stamp, randomly print the same design in different colors to create an overall pattern. (For the slipcover in the photo, the designer used a 2½×5-inch Noel stamp and six colors of fabric ink and printed about 45 images per 3×5-foot section of cloth.)

3 Let the ink dry, then heat-set by pressing for 30 seconds on the right side, using a pressing cloth between the iron and the fabric. Use a dry iron at the cotton setting. Center the drop cloth over the chair. Position the side, front, and back

hems even with the floor. Tuck the excess fabric into the crevice between the seat cushion and the body of the chair, pushing it down as far as possible. The front corners will drape longer, and the back should hang freely.

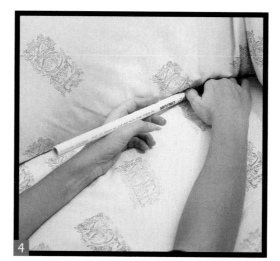

Cut two pieces of plastic pipe 4 inches shorter than the side measurements of the seat and one piece 4 inches shorter than the back measurement of the seat. Slide the plastic pipe down into the crevice between the cushion and body of

the chair, pushing it down as far as you can to help hold the slipcover in place.

5 Thread the needle with 1 yard of ribbon. At seat height of one front corner, gather the excess fabric in your hand. Just behind the gathers, push the needle through the fabric from one side to the other. Tie the ribbon over the gathers to hold the billowed fabric in place. Repeat for the other side.

drop cloth tips

Before starting any of these projects, read these general tips.

■ To remove sizing and soften the fabric, wash and dry the drop cloths before cutting them.

■ The fabric may shrink considerably, so buy a drop cloth larger than you need for each project.

■ Cut the drop cloths to the sizes you'll need for each project and iron the fabric before stamping.

■ Let the ink dry completely, then heat-set the designs by pressing with a dry iron. If you're working with large pieces such as a sofa slipcover, it may be easier to have a dry cleaner press the fabric for you.

■ Always wash and dry the stamp before switching from one ink color to another; otherwise, the ink colors will be muddy, and the stamp will become blurry. Use an old toothbrush and warm tap water to clean the stamps.

■ Use fabric markers to touch up any areas that did not stamp well or to fill in gaps in the borders of the swag and floorcloth.

■ Hem cut edges by machine or turn them under and fuse them in place with fusible hemming tape.

■ Use the drop cloth's hemmed edges as the slipcover's hem whenever possible so you'll have fewer edges to stitch.

■ If you accidentally get fabric ink on carpeting or fabric, blot the area with dishwashing liquid and water, using a clean cloth.

■ If you wiggle the stamp or press too hard and leave inked margins around the image, remove the unwanted ink by carefully dabbing the area with dishwashing liquid and water, using a cotton swab.

ottoman slipcover

here's how...

1 Measure the ottoman as shown in the diagram. Add hem allowances and cut the canvas to these measurements. Hem all raw edges.

2 Using a large stamp, print a single row of one design around the hemline. Alternate colors randomly. Let the ink dry, then heat-set as directed in step 3 of the chair slipcover.

3 Center the canvas over the ottoman. Tie the ribbon around the upper portion of the ottoman. If you like, make the bow fluffier by slipping in snippets of coordinating ribbon.

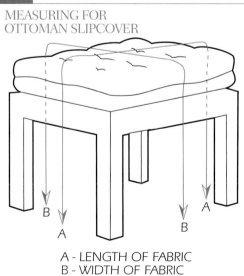

MEASURING FOR
OTTOMAN SLIPCOVER

B
A
A
B

A - LENGTH OF FABRIC
B - WIDTH OF FABRIC

lampshade slipcover

here's how...

1 Measure around the widest part of the shade (usually the bottom). Multiply this measurement by 1½ for the slipcover width. For the depth, measure the lampshade from top to bottom and add 3 inches for the casing, ease, and hem (if needed). Cut out the canvas.

2 Randomly stamp the cloth, alternating colors and designs if you use more than one stamp. Let the ink dry.

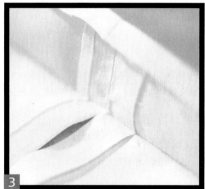

3

Pin the short ends together, right sides facing. Starting at the top, sew down 1½ inches. Leave a 1-inch opening, then sew the remainder of the seam. At the top, press under ¼ inch, then 1¼ inches to form a casing. Topstitch ¼ inch from top folded edge. Sew around the slipcover 1¼ inches from the top folded edge, catching the lower pressed edge and forming the bottom of the casing. Hem the bottom edge of the slipcover if necessary.

4 Thread ribbon through the casing. Slide the slipcover over the lampshade. Adjust the ribbon to fit the top of the shade and tie the ends in a bow.

11

SHOPPING LIST

Materials from shopping list
on page 10 PLUS:
utility weight (5-6 oz.) canvas
runner-style drop cloth
(the design shown is
4×15 feet)
kraft paper

mantel cloth

here's how...

1 Stamp two rows of designs along one long hemmed edge, alternating the colors and designs and placing them in a checkerboard fashion.

2 Drape the cloth across the mantel. Pull it up into swags in several spots, using heavy objects on the mantel to hold the cloth in place.

window scarf

here's how...

1 Protect your work surface with kraft paper that extends several inches beyond the long edge of the canvas.

2 To make the bottom stripe, press the stamp pad against the fabric, making a solid rectangle. Repeat, overlapping the rectangles, until the entire hemline is stamped with a solid stripe. Note: Stripes will be uneven and look hand-done. For a more even stripe, see the directions for the floor cloth.

3 Randomly stamp the designs all over the runner, using at least two stamps and all the colors. The front part of the swag (near the hem stripe) should be more heavily stamped; the back part can be more lightly stamped. Let the ink dry; this may take overnight for the stripe. Heat-set the designs.

4 To hang the swag, loosely loop it over the curtain rod several times. Adjust the fabric so it hangs nicely.

SHOPPING LIST

Materials from shopping list
on page 10 PLUS:
utility weight (5-6 oz.)
runner-style canvas drop
cloth (the design shown
is 4×15 feet

pillows

here's how...

1 For the Button-On Overlay Pillow, pin the two large napkins together, wrong sides facing, and stitch along the hemline, leaving an opening for inserting the pillow form. Slip the pillow inside and stitch the opening closed.

2 For the topper, make a buttonhole in each corner of the cocktail napkin.

3 Center the topper over the pillow and mark the positions for the buttons, then sew one button to each spot.

SHOPPING LIST

2 large napkins
thread to match
pillow or pillow form
For Button-on
  Overlay Pillow:
  coordinating cocktail
  napkin
4 matching buttons
For Grommeted Pillow
  Cover:
grommet tool and
  16 ½-inch grommets
ribbon

For the Grommeted Pillow Cover, use the grommet tool to attach grommets in each corner and along the edges of the napkins, spacing them evenly.

5 Place the napkins with wrong sides facing and holes aligned; lace ribbon through the holes. Insert the pillow and continue lacing; tie the ribbon ends in a bow or knot.

13

hearth rug

here's how...

1 If necessary, cut the floor cloth to the desired size. Place kraft paper over your work surface for protection.

2 Run a strip of artist's tape 1 inch from both long edges of the floor cloth. Run a small piece of rigid plastic (such as a credit card) along the tape to seal the edges to the canvas.

SHOPPING LIST

kraft paper (to protect your
  work surface)
pre-primed floor cloth (from
  an art supply store)
ruler
1-inch-wide artist's or
  painter's tape
small piece of rigid plastic,
  such as a credit card

Press a stamp pad along the exposed edge, creating a stripe. To make the stripe more even, after it is stamped but while the ink is still wet, drag the stamp pad over the damp ink to eliminate overlap marks or uneven spots. Reink the pad as needed. After the ink dries, remove the tape and stamp the short ends in the same manner.

4 After all the borders are dry, create the design stripes in the same way. Measure in 6 inches from the inside edge of the border at each short end. Run a line of tape parallel to the short end. Leave a 1-inch space, then run another line of tape. Repeat to make spaces for six stripes at each end. Stamp the stripes as you did the border stripes.

5 Fill in the center of the floor cloth, if you wish, with stripes or stamped designs; or leave the center blank as shown in the photo on page 9.

SHOPPING LIST

round decorator table
22-inch plywood square
wood screws
plaid and coordinating solid
    fabrics (see steps 2 and 4
    to determine yardage)
thread to match
fusible adhesive tape
    (optional)
1½-inch-wide sheer organdy
    ribbon (see step 5 to
    determine yardage)
¼-inch-wide ribbon

If you have a formal decorating style, choose crisp taffeta and damask for fabric makeovers. Attach a square top to a round decorator table to give yourself more display space.

skirted table

here's how...

1

Working from the underside of the tabletop, attach the 22-inch plywood square to the top of the round decorator table with wood screws.

2 For the skirt top, cut a 23-inch square of plaid fabric. For the sides, cut four 34-inch-wide panels that are long enough to reach the floor, plus 1 inch for seam allowance and hem. Stitch the panels together and make a 2¾-inch-deep pleat at each corner (see the diagram below right).

3 Stitch the top to the sides, using a ½-inch seam. Stitch or fuse the hem.

4 For the topper, cut two 23-inch squares of solid fabric and stitch them together, right sides facing, leaving an opening for turning. Turn, press, and blindstitch the opening closed.

5 Pin 1½-inch-wide sheer organdy ribbon in a crisscross pattern to the topper, then pin narrow satin ribbon over the sheer ribbon. Fold the ribbon ends to the underside of the topper. Glue the ribbons with fabric glue.

15

5 ½"

2 ¾"

2 ¾"

SHOPPING LIST

fabric
thread to match
fusible adhesive tape
coordinating ½-inch-wide
  ribbon

lampshade slipcover

here's how...

Follow the instructions for the stamped lampshade slipcover on page 11. Hem the bottom edge with fusible adhesive tape. Place the slipcover over the lampshade and tie ribbon over the casing.

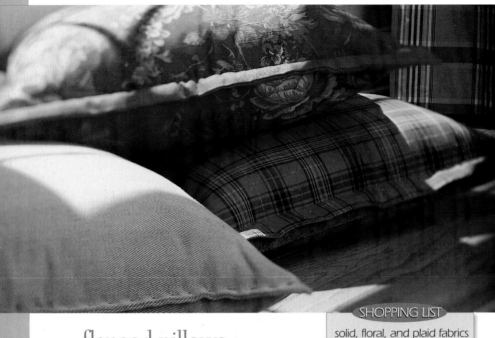

For an overstuffed look, make the pillow cover one size smaller than the pillow form; for example, for a 12-inch sofa pillow, use a 14-inch pillow form.

slipcovered ottoman

here's how...

1 To determine how much fabric you'll need, measure your ottoman as shown in the diagram on page 11. Allow enough additional fabric to cut an 8-inch band for the hem.

2 Cut the fabric to the required size and lay it over the ottoman with the fabric's right side facing you. Use dressmaker's pins to make a pleat at each corner so the slipcover fits the ottoman snugly. Trim the fabric to about 3 inches above the floor.

3 Cut and piece fabric as necessary to make a strip 8 inches wide and long enough to fit all the way around the slipcover's bottom edge. Press the fabric in half lengthwise. Carefully remove the slipcover from the ottoman and pin the the hem band to the slipcover, right sides facing and raw edges aligned. Stitch, using a ½-inch seam allowance. Replace the pins holding the pleats with buttons.

NO-SEW OPTION: Instead of hemming the slipcover with a separate band, add 1 inch to the ottoman measurements for a hem. Secure the hem with fusible adhesive tape, following the manufacturer's instructions.

flanged pillows

here's how...

1 To make the gold herringbone pillow, cut two squares of fabric the size of the pillow form plus 1 inch all around. Place the squares right sides facing and stitch ½ inch from the raw edges, leaving an opening for turning. Make sure the opening is large enough for you to insert the pillow form.

2 Turn the pillowcase right side out and press the edges. Insert the pillow form and blindstitch the opening closed. To make the flange, hand-sew a running stitch ½ inch from the edges, using rust-colored embroidery floss and an embroidery needle.

3 For the floral pillow, cut two squares of fabric the size of the pillow form plus 2 inches all around. With right sides facing, stitch the squares together, using a ½-inch seam allowance and leaving an opening for turning and stuffing.

4 Turn and press; stitch 1½ inches from the edges to create the flange, leaving an opening for stuffing. Fill the pillowcase with polyester fiberfill, then

5

finish stitching the flange. Turn under the raw edges on the pillow edging and blindstitch the opening closed.

For the plaid pillow, cut two squares of fabric the size of the pillow form plus 3¾ inches all around. Fold under 1⅞ inches on each side and press. Place the two squares with wrong sides facing and mark the stitching line 1¾ inches from the edges. Stitch, leaving an opening for inserting the pillow form. Press to give the flanges a crisp edge. Insert the pillow form or stuff the pillow with polyester fiberfill. Machine-stitch the opening closed.

16

18

A display on a buffet or mantel helps set a holiday mood. It also suggests a feeling of formality or informality, depending on the way you arrange the elements. Symmetrical arrangements create a formal look because they convey stability, order, and classical harmony. To achieve symmetry, draw an imaginary line down the center of your display space and then arrange objects in a mirror-image fashion on each side of the line.

Asymmetry is trickier because things don't match on either side of the center dividing line, but the grouping still should be balanced visually. Asymmetrical groupings feel more dynamic, active, and exciting, but even though they're not as formal as symmetrical arrangements, they can be quite elegant nevertheless.

design *lesson*

symmetry

To produce a symmetrical arrangement like the one on page 18, think in pairs: two tall silver vases, two silver goblets, two crystal candleholders. Arrange flowers and greenery in the vases in a fanlike spray; this is a classic shape that works well with tall, trumpet-shaped containers. Insert short pieces of fir in the goblets to make a collar of greenery, and rest a tall sugar pinecone on each. The pinecone supplies a vertical element shorter than the arrangements but taller than the candles.

Place the arrangements on each side of the imaginary center line. To keep the display from being static and boring, give it depth by standing the goblets in front of the arrangements and the candles toward the back. Also overlap elements slightly to lead the eye across the design from the lowest point to the highest and back down again in a fan-shaped arc. To tie the vases together visually, rest a low bowl of pears between them and trail sheer ribbon along the buffet.

asymmetry

You can use the same pairs of objects to create an asymmetrical display, too; just add books or boxes to provide different levels, and avoid setting up mirror images. Instead of a fan-shaped arc, think of a triangle with sides of unequal length. Raise one flower arrangement on a stack of books to mark the highest point. Place the second arrangement on the sideboard, at the imaginary center line or just to the other side of it.

To anchor the lowest point of the grouping, rest a candlestick on books

and couple it with one of the silver goblets. Raising the candlestick gives it greater visual weight, and pairing two smaller objects balances the apparent visual weight of the taller flower arrangement. To supply variety, replace the goblet's sugar pinecone with a pear and place the pinecone in the low bowl with greenery. The bowl, resting at the imaginary center line at the front of the display, helps balance the taller side.

To anchor the display on the right, place the second goblet and the remaining candlestick on that side, toward the back. Your eye should step up from the candle to the cone to the arrangement, then follow the line down to the lowest point and around to the front. Sheer ribbon curling in and out around the base of the arrangement also will help lead the eye in and out across the display.

Here's how to create formal and informal displays for a sideboard or mantel and how to tweak them for seasonal change.

Designed for Change

ↀWhether you prefer symmetrical or asymmetrical design, you can build in options for change by starting with a few basic elements and adding seasonal accents.

autumn

Start with a large serving tray and a cachepot or vase filled with florist's foam as the foundation for all three centerpieces. (Look for florist's foam at crafts stores and florist's supply shops. You'll need to replace the foam for each arrangement.) For autumn, spread a tablecloth or runner in neutral or fall colors along the sideboard, then rest the tray on top of it. Fill the cachepot with fresh chrysanthemums, birch twigs, cattails, dried hydrangeas, and fall leaves in a simple, fan-shaped arrangement. Mound gourds, winter squash, and miniature pumpkins on the tray, allowing them to spill over onto the sideboard.

For a softer look, tuck pads of reindeer moss around the cachepot and among the gourds at the edge of the tray. Insert stems of flowers into florist's water vials (from a florist's supply shop or crafts store). Slip the vials among the gourds to add some horizontal lines at the base of the display. Bringing the flowers down among the gourds also helps tie the flower arrangement to the base visually.

Stand pillar candles and candlesticks on each side of the display. Use large, sturdy dried leaves as wax catchers for the pillars.

21

22

christmas

To shift the design toward an elegant holiday look, replace the autumn table runner with one in rich reds and golds. Remove the winter squash and miniature pumpkins, and spray-paint the gourds with a mixture of copper and silver. (For a richer color effect, apply the second color while the first is still wet.)

Save the dried hydrangeas for a winter arrangement, and spray-paint the birch twigs white. Using the painted birch twigs as a starting point, create a new arrangement with fresh caspia, apricot-colored roses (to pick up the copper color), and fresh evergreens. Arrange branches of evergreens along the runner as well as on the tray, and rest the painted gourds and pinecones on the greenery. Tuck in the moss as for the autumn design, and thread a garland of small ornaments through the flower arrangement. Keep the pillar candles in place, but add one candlestick on each side for a more formal look.

winter

After Christmas, change the arrangement for a more
wintry look for New Year's and the weeks following by
shifting the color scheme to cool green and snowy
white. Replace the Christmas runner with a crisp white
crocheted one, and remove the evergreens and spray-
painted gourds. Keep the pinecones, moss, caspia, and
birch twigs and bring back the dried hydrangeas saved
from the autumn arrangement.

Make a new arrangement of caspia, birch twigs, and
hydrangeas, adding white carnations to emphasize the
winter theme. Mound moss and pinecones on the tray
around the cachepot, and add carnations and lengths of
ivy, inserting the stem ends in florist's vials to keep the
ivy and flowers fresh. Replace the pillar candles with
crystal votive candleholders and white tea lights. Leave
the candlesticks on each side of the display to maintain
the formal look.

Give paperwhite narcissus a ground cover of red cranberries for a merry accent in a foyer, kitchen, or living room. Four to six weeks before you want blooms, plant bulbs on gravel in a shallow bowl. Water as needed, keeping the water level just below the bottom of the bulbs. Cover the gravel with cranberries when you're ready to display the flowers.

In a Twinkling:
Festive Touches

Accent your favorite print or painting with a big bow stitched from fabric. Make the bow from a 37×17-inch strip folded in half lengthwise and stitched into a tube. Turn the tube right side out and stitch the short ends together, then wrap a 4×8-inch strip around the center of the loop for a knot. Make the tails from 17×41-inch strips folded in half lengthwise and stitched. Turn right side out and pin them to the back of the knot.

String large wooden beads, pecans or walnuts, and dried pomegranates on dental floss to make garlands for hanging from bedposts. Use an electric drill with a 1/16-inch bit to pierce the pomegranates and nuts from side to side. With a large tapestry needle, thread them on the dental floss.

◀ Supplement decorations with red and white accessories. Emphasize the Christmas colors in stockings, package wraps, and tree ornaments with simple touches, such as red flowers in white vases, red apples on a white dish, red and white accent pillows, and simple white valances trimmed with red rickrack or ribbon.

▶ Guarantee your guests sweet holiday dreams with a simple swag of fresh cedar tied across the headboard. Their very own Christmas tree also adds festive fragrance. The tree need not be elaborate: Plant a small tree in wet sand in a galvanized metal bucket, then hang miniature ornaments from the branches.

◀ Fluff up a room with homespun holiday pillows. Stitch squares of white or green felt, wool, or cotton; use crewel yarn and a running stitch to make crisscross, snowflake, and 'Noel' designs. Make the dots on the Noel pillow with satin stitches.

With just a few ordinary elements, you can create an elegant and welcoming display in the foyer.

dramatic

entrance

In the spirit of "use what you have" decorating, put silver coffee urns, teapots, and sugar bowls to work as vases for flowers and candy canes; fill a silver bowl with red pears for more color. Lay an artificial wreath on the table and nestle a couple of small potted azaleas in the center. Then rest yellow apples around the wreath and add yellow-green bows for a bright accent. To dress up the mirror, buy several yards of red fabric and drape it over the top. For the candy cane crest, bundle canes together with florist's tape. Tie a bow over the tape to hide it, then wire the bundle to the mirror.

Hang these ornaments on your tree—or from the chandelier or windows—for festive sparkle.

tree jewelry

SHOPPING LIST

(for 3 ornaments)
adhesive tape
hole punch
From a fabric store:
Coats & Clark metallic
   sewing thread, ART.D62
   #808
⅓ yard clear plastic vinyl
pinking shears or decorative-
   edge scissors
From a crafts store:
9 yards of Kreinik Metallics
   Medium Braid (#16) in
   green, purple, blue,
   and gold
embroidery needle
   (should have an eye large
   enough for the braid yet
   small enough to go
   through beads)
multicolor glass Rochaille
   "E" Beads 6/0
multicolored
   metallic confetti

28

Confetti Ornaments

here's how...

1 Cut the metallic braid into nine 1-yard lengths. Thread the needle with one length of braid and knot one end. Thread 8 to 10 inches with beads. Remove the needle, knot the other end of the braid, and push half of the beads toward each end of the braid. Repeat for the remaining eight lengths of the braid.

2 Pin together three beaded braids, keeping half of the beads at each end. Plait the braids together between the beaded ends. Knot just above the beads. Repeat for each group of three braids.

3 Enlarge the patterns on page 31 at 240 percent on a photocopier. Cut out.

4 Cut six 6-inch squares of vinyl. Place about 1 tablespoon of confetti in the center of one square. Place the second square of vinyl on top of the first, sandwiching the confetti in between.

5 Center a paper pattern under the vinyl sandwich. Use adhesive tape to hold the pattern in place.

6 Thread a sewing machine with metallic sewing thread both on top and in the bobbin. Place the vinyl sandwich, paper side down, under the presser foot. Using the paper pattern as a guide, stitch ¼ inch in from the paper edge through the vinyl and the paper. Remove the ornament from the sewing machine. Cut around the edges of the paper pattern with pinking shears and carefully tear the paper away from the stitching.

7 Use a hole punch to make a hole in the top and bottom of the ornament. Fold the beaded braid in half. Thread it through the bottom punched hole and knot it about 3 inches from the fold. Thread the folded end through the top punched hole to serve as the hanger.

20 feet of 22-gauge round
  nickel wire (or use 22-
  gauge copper or
  brass wire)
needle-nose pliers
½-inch diameter dowel
4½x6-inch sheet of
  white cotton linter for
  making paper (from a
  crafts store)
blender
container that is wide and
  deep enough to
  submerge the wire
  ornament
silver glitter fabric paint
  and/or clear spray acrylic
  varnish (optional)
18 inches of 1½-inch-wide
  silver sheer wire ribbon
1 yard of ⅜-inch wide
  silver wire ribbon
(For ordering information,
  see page 158.)

Curly Wire Christmas Ball

29

here's how...

1 To make the hanging loop, begin about 2 inches from one end of the length of wire, and wrap the wire around the dowel. Use the needle-nose pliers to twist the wire to make a loop. Remove the loop from the dowel.

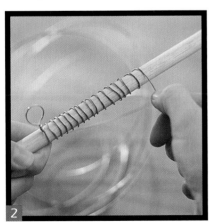

2 Place the loop at the left end of the dowel and just above the dowel. Wrap the wire tightly around the dowel. Remove the coiled wire and stretch the coil into a 1-yard length.

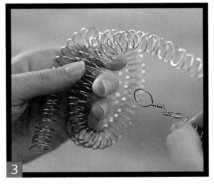

Beginning at the end opposite the hanging loop, wrap the coil around your hand as if you were wrapping ribbon to make a bow. Remove the wrapped wire and pull the hanging loop through the middle. Shape the wire until you have a nice ball shape.

4 To frost the wire ball, tear the cotton linter into 1-inch pieces. Place half of the torn linter in your blender and fill the blender with water. Blend on high for about two minutes, using short bursts to keep the blender from overheating, until the mixture is smooth and creamy.

5 Pour the pulp into the container. Clean the blender thoroughly, but don't pour any excess pulp down the drain. Instead, pour it outside in the garden, where it can decompose.

6 Stir the water to bring the paper pulp to the top. Holding the ornament by the loop, dip it into the paper pulp, then hang the ornament over a protected surface to let it dry. For a thicker coat of paper, repeat the dipping and drying.

7 If desired, lightly brush the ornament with fabric glitter paint and spray with clear acrylic varnish.

8 Fold 18 inches of the 1½-inch-wide ribbon in half. From 24 inches of the ⅜-inch-wide ribbon, make a bow. Center the folded ribbon behind the hanging loop and position the bow over the base of the hanging loop. Tie the ribbon and the bow to the base of the hanging loop, using the remaining ⅜-inch-wide ribbon.

ornament patterns

for Confetti Ornaments, page 28

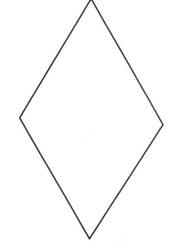

ENLARGE
PATTERNS
240%

Beaded-Wire Ornaments

reindeer

here's how...

1 Cut a 26-inch length of beading wire. Wrap one end around a toothpick to make a tiny loop (this keeps the beads from falling off the wire).

2 String beads onto the wire to within about ¾ inch of the end.

3 Using the photo as a pattern, start with the front antler and bend the beaded wire to outline the deer shape. Twist at the tail and legs to define these parts of the shape. Twist the antlers around each other to hold them in place at the top of the head.

4 Hang with a length of gold cord.

celtic knot

here's how...

1 Cut a 27-inch length of #28 gauge wire. Wrap one end around a toothpick to make a tiny loop for the knot.

2 String red and orange beads onto the wire, changing colors randomly.

SHOPPING LIST

From a crafts store or bead-supply shop:

FOR REINDEER:
#28 gauge silver beading wire
Style 140 gold Rochaille beads
gold thread or cord

FOR CELTIC KNOT:
#28 gauge silver beading wire
Style 140 Rochaille beads in red and orange
#34 gauge silver beading wire
gold thread or cord

3 Twist the wire ends together, then fold the loop in half and twist to form one twisted length of beads.

4 Using a small piece of wire, join the ends of the twisted length to form a circle.

5 Using the photo as a pattern, bend and shape the beaded circle to make the knot. Use #34 gauge wire to tie the overlaps together.

6 Hang with a length of gold cord.

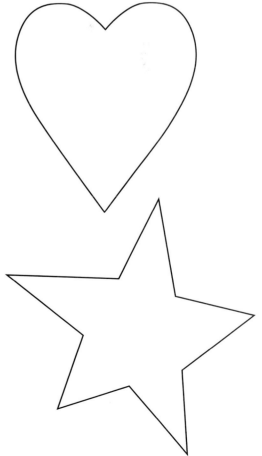

Let your tree reflect your decorating style—elegant, natural, or homespun.

trio of *trees*

Winter White

For a lush, glittering look, choose five or six basic types of ornaments and collect several boxes of each. Here, the wardrobe includes gold, silver, and white balls in different sizes; snowflakes; twiggy silver stars; white pinecones; silver reindeer; and silver pendants. With an array like this, you'll have variety for an interesting tree with enough repetition to create a unified look. Put on the lights first, then distribute each type of ornament evenly, tucking some deep into the tree and hanging others at the branch tips. Add a few specialty ornaments in the same color scheme, and tuck sprigs of holly among the branches for contrasting texture. For the finishing touch, drape a beaded garland around the tree in even swags.

To warm up the silver-and-white combination, add fresh greenery and gilded pears. Use spray paint or metal leaf (from a crafts store) to gild fresh or artificial pears. For a softer gold, brush the gilded pear with brown acrylic paint, quickly wiping off most of the paint so it tones down the color but doesn't cover it. (Fresh pears aren't suitable for eating after they've been gilded.)

leafy tree skirt

Cut a circle of the desired diameter from plum-color quilted fabric. Use a real leaf to make a pattern for the fabric leaves, then cut enough leaves from celery-green felt to ring the edge of the skirt. Use fabric glue to secure the leaves, overlapping them as shown and allowing half of the shape to extend beyond the skirt's edge.

Naturally Yours

Take your cue from the garden for decorations. Shop crafts stores for small decorative birdhouses and bird nests, twig stars, and pepperberries to hang on the branches. To make a fluffy garland, wire broadleaf evergreens or florist's greenery such as eucalyptus, ruscus, or smilax to jute twine, using paddle wire. Drape the garland on the branches like a feather boa. Topiaries on the mantel reinforce the garden theme.

Fresh & Simple

❧ For a clean, pared-down, yet homespun look, choose just a few types of ornaments with simple shapes. Make sure one group is large enough to provide emphasis, like the handmade burlap stars here. Give large ornaments room to hang by choosing a tree with short needles and sturdy, well-separated branches. Noble fir or spruces are best for this kind of display.

SHOPPING LIST
two 8-inch squares of burlap
   in ivory or tan
6-inch length of jute
matching thread
polyester fiberfill
pinking shears

burlap puffy star

here's how...

1 Draw a star that measures 6 inches from tip to tip. Cut out the pattern and transfer it to one burlap square.

2 With wrong sides facing and the ends of the 6-inch length of jute inserted at the top of the star, stitch the burlap squares together along the pattern outline, leaving an opening for stuffing.

3 Stuff the star lightly with fiberfill and stitch the opening closed. Use pinking shears to trim the fabric to within ¼ inch of the seam lines, being careful not to cut the hanger.

ball ornaments

here's how...

1 To make the white, paper-wrapped balls, cut a square of tissue paper about 5 inches larger than a ball's diameter. Center the ball on the paper. Wrap the paper around the ball, twisting both ends like a candy wrapper.

2

Trim the excess paper just above the twist. Secure the twisted paper with pins.

3

Wrap jute around the balls as desired, securing it with plain or white-headed pins. Pin a loop hanger at the top.

4 To make the twine-covered balls, spread glue in a 1½-inch circle on a plastic foam ball. Pin the end of the jute twine at the center of the circle, then coil the jute around the center. Continue gluing and coiling until you've covered the ball. To make stripes, alternate between jute and cotton twine. Hold the ends of the twine in place with plain straight pins until the glue is nearly dry, then remove the pins. Attach a loop for hanging at the top.

SHOPPING LIST

2- to 5-inch diameter plastic foam balls
white tissue paper
plain and white-headed straight pins
jute twine
cotton twine
white crafts glue

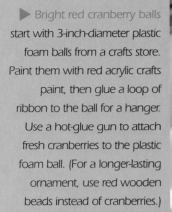

▶ Bright red cranberry balls start with 3-inch-diameter plastic foam balls from a crafts store. Paint them with red acrylic crafts paint, then glue a loop of ribbon to the ball for a hanger. Use a hot-glue gun to attach fresh cranberries to the plastic foam ball. (For a longer-lasting ornament, use red wooden beads instead of cranberries.)

In a Twinkling:
Ornaments

◀ Turn a marble collection into ornaments with mechanic's wire from a hardware store. Use 16-gauge wire for large marbles and 18-gauge for small ones. Wrap a 12-inch length of wire around a large marking pen to make a cradle for the marble. Twist the wire into smaller coils above and below the cradle and bend one end of the wire to make a hook for hanging. Push the marble into the cradle and shape the wire as necessary to hold the marble securely in place.

◀ Jingle all the way with a large sleigh bell ornament dressed up with red canella berries and evergreen sprigs. Wire the berries (available at crafts stores) to the greenery, then wire the bouquet to the hanging loop of the bell. Use narrow ribbon to tie the bell to the tree or to a doorknob.

▼ Turn the metal rings from canning jar lids into photo-frame ornaments. Wrap jute tightly and evenly around the ring until the metal is completely covered, then glue the ends to the back of the ring. Or use low-temperature hot glue to attach colored beads and alphabet beads, one or two at a time, around the inside of the ring. Cover the outside edge of the ring with ribbon. Trim a photo to fit the ring and glue it to the back. Glue a ribbon loop to the back (flat side) for a hanger.

▲ Look for miniature pails in crafts stores. Tuck in kumquats and a sprig of red berries for a quick handmade ornament.

Enhance traditional celebrations with handmade accessories and festive touches.

decorating *for* hanukkah

Focus attention on the stories and traditions of Hanukkah with a tabletop or mantel display of six-pointed stars, Hanukkah gelt, and dreidels. Bring out pillows just for the holiday to accent a sofa or chairs. Judah Maccabee inspired the appliqué pillow on page 42. Use a Hanukkah stamp and fabric dyes to make the tone-on-tone pillow.

Mantel

Make a quick mantel scarf from sheer silver and blue napkins (or cut squares from organdy fabric and hem the edges). Embellish one corner of each napkin with a crystal bead and a foil-wrapped chocolate coin.

To attach the coin, use an embroidery needle to thread metallic embroidery thread or fine gold cording through the coin near the edge. To draw the cord ends through the bead, use a plastic dental floss threader (look for this in discount stores and drug stores where dental floss is sold); push it through the bead, insert the cord ends, then pull them through. In one corner of the napkin, work the threads apart with a needle and push the cord ends through; knot them on the wrong side. Fold the napkins on the diagonal and layer them on the mantel as a base for a dreidel collection and Hanukkah gelt.

Maccabee Pillow

here's how...

1 Enlarge the soldier patterns on a photocopier by 200 percent and cut them out. Also transfer the patterns for the armor, collar, and shield to sandpaper and cut them out. Trim the seam allowances from the sandpaper pieces.

2 Following the manufacturer's instructions, iron the fusible adhesive material to the wrong side of the tan, burgundy, and brown suedelike fabrics. Cut the face, arm, and legs from tan; cut the tunic and headband from burgundy and the hair, beard, mustache, eyebrows, belt, and shoes from brown. Cut out the armor, collar, and shield from gold lamé. Draw the eyes and nose on the face using the permanent marker.

3 Place the lamé pieces facedown,

and center the corresponding sandpaper piece on each, rough side down. Clip the curves to the edge of the sandpaper; using an iron, press the seam allowances over the sandpaper. The fabric won't slip, and you'll get a perfect curved edge.

4 Cut the denim to measure 16½×56 inches. Fold the strip in half to find the middle, then open the fabric. Draw lines with the dressmaker's chalk 10¼ inches from each side of the middle; these will be the top and bottom edges of the pillow front. Draw another line 2¼ inches in from these edges to mark the top and bottom of the image area; also mark the sides about 2¾ inches from each raw edge.

5 Center the tunic inside the image area, then place the head, leg, and arm pieces to check for positioning. When you're satisfied, fuse the pattern pieces in this order: tunic, face, headband, beard, mustache, hair, eyebrows; arm, legs, shoes. Place the arm and leg pieces so the edges are flush with the tunic, rather than overlapping them. Using gold metallic thread, topstitch the collar and armor in place over the tunic. Fuse the belt over the lamé at the waist.

6 Place a small amount of polyester fiberfill in the center of the area where the shield will go, then pin the shield in place. Topstitch close to the edge and again ¼ inch from the first line of stitching.

7 Stitch gold seed beads along the armhole of the armor and around the shield between the lines of stitching. Use fabric glue to attach gold ribbon as trim on the sleeve and skirt of the tunic. Cut the leather shoelace into pieces and glue them to the feet and legs as shown.

8 With the appliquéd figure facing you, fold the short ends of the denim fabric piece toward the middle along the chalk lines, overlapping them to make a fabric envelope about 16×21½ inches. Fold under the raw edges on the short ends, then stitch the long sides. Turn the pillow cover right side out. Topstitch around the rectangle 2¼ inches in from the outside edge to create a flange.

9 Use fabric glue to adhere narrow gold ribbon over the flange stitching. Glue the purple ribbon to the flange close to the gold ribbon to make a frame. Stuff the pillow with polyester fiberfill.

Make a square pillow using your favorite pattern or one of the methods on page 16. Then use rubber stamps and light blue permanent fabric paint to decorate the cover. (See page 158 for a mail-order source for stamps and paints.)

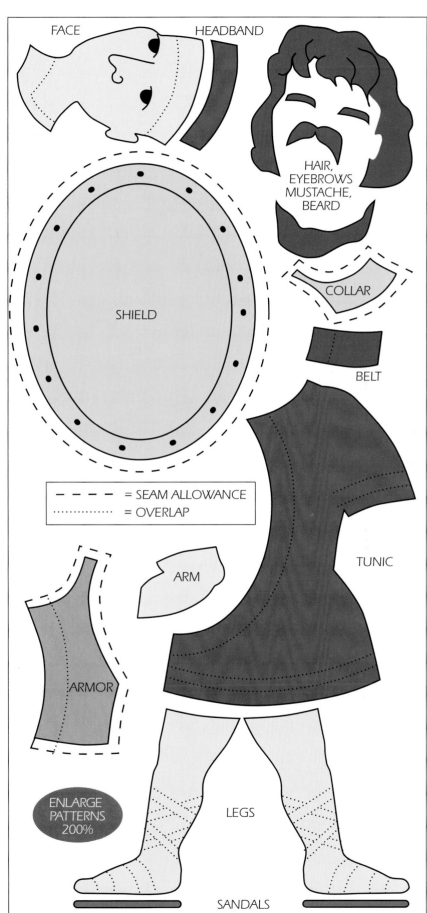

FACE HEADBAND

HAIR, EYEBROWS MUSTACHE, BEARD

COLLAR

BELT

SHIELD

- - - - - = SEAM ALLOWANCE
.... = OVERLAP

TUNIC

ARM

ARMOR

LEGS

ENLARGE PATTERNS 200%

SANDALS

43

An arrangement of fruits and vegetables in an all-white scheme puts a new spin on the harvest theme. Look for white or neutral-color produce, such as cauliflower, ornamental kale, honeydew melons, elephant garlic, fennel, cabbages, miniature pumpkins, and wheat. Prop a garden trug or shallow basket up against the wall for a strong vertical element.

In a Twinkling: Mantels

For white-on-white simplicity, scour flea markets for a picture frame with wide molding and paint it with flat white latex house paint. Place it just off center on the mantel and balance it with a white garden urn—you can use an old iron one or a new plaster replica. Scatter gold and silver balls and white votive candles for sparkly accents.

Delight children (or your own inner child) with a mantel in a toyland theme. If you have a collection of vintage toys, this is the perfect opportunity to show them off. Or let your children or grandchildren help you decorate the mantel, using some of their favorite toys. Below the shelf, hang fresh greenery from cup hooks or small nails. Attach toys, small packages, and a doll or favorite stuffed animal to the garland with floral wire.

Set a playful mood with a gingerbread family and oversized felt stockings along the mantel shelf. Buy gingerbread cookies from a bakery and decorate them yourself, or make your own with your favorite gingerbread recipe. The boy and girl cookies were cut with 5-inch and 7½-inch cutters, and the largest cookies were cut out using a 12-inch pattern. To make a pattern, trace an ordinary cookie cutter onto a sheet of paper and enlarge it on a photocopier to the desired size. Use the enlarged shape as a pattern to cut from well-chilled dough that you've rolled directly onto the baking pan. Decorate the cookies with purchased tubes of decorator icing.

45

Welcome winter with a snowy theme using scarves, mittens, and snow gear you won't be needing for a few weeks. A snuggly wool lap blanket or layers of wool scarves serve as a base. Rest ice skates, snow globes, family photos, and any other snow-related items you might have on top. Pin crocheted snowflakes to the fabric and hang mittens, using clips made from suspender clasps.

Capture winter light with a collection of mirrors. Mix flea market finds with new mirrors in a variety of sizes and shapes, placing the largest or tallest ones at the back and layering the small and medium-size ones in front. Add sparkly ornaments and candles for festive reflections.

Explore your family's cultural heritage and add some of those old customs to enrich your own decorations and celebrations.

christmas
traditions

Sinterklaas

Although the saint known as Nicholas was originally a priest and later a bishop in 4th-century Turkey, he came to be the patron saint of a surprising assortment of groups—fishermen, sailors, virgins, children, pawnbrokers, and the country of Russia all claimed him. His church in Demre, Turkey, became a popular destination for pilgrims in the Middle Ages. Eventually, he became the patron saint of Amsterdam as well.

According to Dutch tradition, Sinterklaas, his servant Piet, and many helpers arrive by boat on December 5 (Sinderklaas Eve). Mounted on a white horse, Sinterklaas rides over the rooftops, listening in to check on children's behavior. Wooden shoes filled with carrots or hay for the horse are left by the fireplace. In the homes of good children, Piet takes the treats and leaves behind a small gift or candy.

Sinderklaas Eve and Sinderklaas Day (December 6) are days of festivity and merriment—including jokes, rhymes, simple gifts in strange wrappings, parties, and general celebration. Traditional foods are spice cookies, hot chocolate, apple fritters, Dutch doughnuts, and Dutch letters.

Because St. Nicholas was known for his good deeds, the Dutch in some areas observe December 5 and 6 as special days for exchanging gifts with family and friends. It's also a time for sharing with the poor.

This hearthside decoration recalls the treats left for Sinterklaas's horse, but replaces the hay with wheat, which is readily available at crafts stores.

hearthside decoration
here's how...

1 Slide several handfuls of blonde and blackbeard wheat into the shoes, trimming the stem ends so the heads extend 6 to 10 inches beyond the shoes. Trim the greens of the carrots on the diagonal so they are 3 to 5 inches long. Tuck several carrots into each shoe. Arrange the shoes as shown here.

2 String the bells on the ribbon so they resemble sleigh bells. Place the fruit, ribbon and bells, and vintage items around, between, and behind the shoes. Be sure to keep the arrangement away from any flames or embers.

Russian Customs

Celebrations in Russia today may occur on one of three different dates, depending on the family's religion and traditions—December 25, January 1, or January 7 (Russian Orthodox). The most common is January 1, which is the New Year's celebration.

Although the Soviets originally banned all celebrations, they later reconsidered and declared New Year's Day a holiday. Many of the old traditions and rituals that could be separated from religious content were revived. These included the Yolka (a decorated fir tree), Ded Moroz (Grandfather Frost), and Snegurochka (his granddaughter). Ded Moroz would bring the tree into the family's home at night and decorate it so when the children awoke on New Year's Day, the tree was a glorious surprise. Today, the family usually decorates the tree beforehand, using fruits, figures made out of fruits, paper or glass ornaments, and painted or carved folk crafts. Traditional Russian symbols such as eggs and matroyska dolls often are used on the tree as well.

The eggs shown here were inspired by the jeweled Fabergé eggs commissioned by the Czar as gifts for special occasions, including Christmas.

fabergé eggs

here's how...

1 Using an awl, make a small hole in the small and large ends of each egg. Slide a skewer through the egg to use as a handle while you work on it. Paint the eggs with one or two coats of acrylic paint in the desired colors.

47

2 Referring to the photo for guidance, draw simple geometric shapes, such as grids, diamonds, or scallops, onto the eggs. For glitter eggs, draw along the lines with dimensional glitter paint. For foiled eggs, place the adhesive in a squeeze bottle and apply it along the lines. Apply the foil according to the manufacturer's directions.

3 After the glitter or foiling dries, erase any visible pencil lines. Glue the gems and filigree caps in place. Remove the skewer. Glue a necklace finding to each end, making sure the opening of the finding aligns with the hole in the egg. Run wire through the egg. At the large end, loop it around the loop of a tassel and pull the tassel loop up into the egg. At the other end, loop the wire back on itself to create a hanging loop and to hold the wire tightly in place.

SHOPPING LIST

- awl
- wooden skewers
- papier-mâché eggs (5-inch size)
- acrylic paint in the desired colors
- disposable foam brushes
- dimensional glitter paint
- dimensional gold foiling with a squeeze bottle for adhesive, such as Anita's Gold Foiling kit
- assorted glue-on gems, filigree bead caps, and other embellishments
- necklace finding or end cap for end
- thick white crafts glue or hot glue gun and glue sticks
- gold wire or fabric-covered wire
- small tassels

Select a set of numerals from an alphabet style book (from art supply and bookstores). Copy the numerals to make numbers 1 through 12, then cut the numbers apart and tape them to another sheet of paper with plenty of space around each number. Photocopy that paper onto the desired color of paper for the numbered tags.

The 12 Days of Christmas

48

This English counting song, which can help pass the time on long driving trips, has been part of our popular musical tradition for generations. Some people believe that it was written in the 1500s as a coded catechism for teaching the Catholic faith. Religion and politics were inextricably linked in 16th-century Europe, and when Catholics lost control of the English crown after Queen Mary's death, they also lost the freedom to practice their faith openly.

The verses of the song are said to symbolize elements of basic doctrine, although in fact there's nothing in the elements that the Church of England would have argued with. Today, the interpretation can add a spiritual dimension to what otherwise may seem simply whimsical.

The period of Twelve Days (observed by many Protestants as well as Roman Catholics) starts on December 26 and ends January 6, when the Three Wise Men arrived at the manger. Have some fun this year by using the song as the starting point for family activities. To make each day really special, package a small gift in its own themed gift box to leave beside each person's plate at breakfast or dinner.

general box wrapping instructions:

here's how...

Cut pieces of the desired paper ½ to ¾ inch larger than the top and bottom of the box. Place the bottom paper face-down; center the box bottom on it. Fold the long sides up and over the edge to the inside of the box and tape or glue in place. At the ends, fold the paper up, then crease the excess paper at the corners along the diagonal. Unfold the paper and press the diagonal crease in toward the end of the box. Refold the paper to the inside, pressing the fold at the corner of the box; tape or glue in place inside the box.

On the first day of Christmas my true love gave to me a partridge in a pear tree.

The pear tree is said to symbolize the cross; the partridge, Jesus Christ, because a mother partridge risks her own life to save her chicks by luring predators away from the nest.

here's how...

To make this gift box, wrap a small box top and bottom with old sheet music, then layer and wrap rice paper over the sheet music. Glue velvet millinery leaves and a miniature artificial pear to the top. Trim the number label to the desired size and glue in place beneath the leaves.

activities

Partridge may be hard to find in your local supermarket, but pears abound. Buy a couple of each kind and combine them with cheeses (see pages 64–71 for suggestions), some fresh bread, figs, and other fresh fruit. Serve with wine, sparkling juice, or tea for a European-style lunch or dinner.

and glue the ends together to make loops. Glue the pieces together into a rosette. Cut the number label into a circle with pinking shears to fit just inside the rosette. Add two 1½-inch ribbon streamers and glue to the box top.

activities

Try a new recipe for chicken at one of today's meals. Or try Cornish hens or a game bird.

On the fourth day of Christmas my true love gave to me four calling birds.

The calling birds represent the four Evangelists, Matthew, Mark, Luke, and John, and their Gospel accounts.

here's how...

1 For this box, start with a 6-inch-diameter unfinished circular birch bandbox from a crafts store. Glue flat upholstery braid around the rim of the lid. Coil gold snowflake garland (from a party supply store) into a 5-inch-diameter circle and glue it to the box lid for the wreath.

2 Glue four small artificial birds (from a crafts store) around the wreath, spacing them evenly. Glue small pinecones between each pair of birds, spraying some of the cones silver before gluing them. Weave narrow wire-edge ribbon through the wreath. For the number tag, trim the number label to the desired size and glue it in place.

activities

Telephone at least four friends you've been meaning to contact but just haven't gotten around to calling. (E-mail doesn't count!) If they're not home, leave a message on the answering machine to let them know you're thinking of them.

On the second day of Christmas my true love gave to me two turtle doves.

The doves stand for the Old and New Testaments, but also may represent the doves that were required as an offering when a male child was dedicated in the Temple at the age of 12.

here's how...

1 Glue satin ribbon around the sides of a round box (about 4 inches in diameter); set aside. Trace the box lid onto a color print of doves (from a bird book, a greeting card, or gift paper). Cut out, adding ¼ inch all around. Glue the print to the box lid with matte medium; clip the excess ¼ inch to the edge of the lid, then fold and glue the flaps to the sides of the lid. Glue upholstery trim around the edge of the top to cover the flaps.

2 For the number tag, cut the label into a circle and cover a 1-inch-diameter button form as you would with fabric. Twist narrow ribbon into a rosette slightly larger than the number button and glue to the button back. Clip the ends of a ribbon scrap into a V, then glue to the edge of the lid. Glue the rosette on the ribbon.

activities

Doves represent peace, so during the family dinner make a list of ways to spread peace in your corner of the world. These can range from reducing conflicts between the kids to reaching a quiet solution to a school or work problem.

On the third day of Christmas my true love gave to me three french hens.

Threes usually symbolize the Trinity but also may stand for the theological virtues of faith, hope, and charity.

here's how...

1 Wrap the bottom of a small cardboard box with fabric, using a drop of hot glue to secure the edges inside the box. Sponge-paint the box lid with coordinating acrylic paints.

2 Have a copy shop make a color copy of a clip-art print of hens, using red ink only. Cut out the image and glue it to the top of the lid with matte acrylic medium. Apply a coat of medium to the entire lid.

3 For the number label ribbon, cut four 2-inch lengths of ¼-inch-wide ribbon. Fold

49

50

On the fifth day of Christmas my true love gave to me five golden rings.

These are said to represent the first five books of the Old Testament, often referred to as the Pentateuch.

here's how...

Start with a purchased gold box. Slip five gold-color plastic rings (available from crafts stores) onto ¾-inch-wide purple velvet ribbon; then wrap the ribbon around the box, gluing the ends in place. Trim the number label and glue in place.

activities

Give each family member five strips of yellow or gold paper. Have them write the following, one on each strip.

1. their favorite thing that happened this Christmas season

2. their favorite memory of last Christmas

3. their favorite Christmas ever

4. their funniest Christmas memory

5. one thing they hope to accomplish before next Christmas

Staple the strips into circles, joining them into a paper chain. Use the chain to decorate the Christmas tree, a stairway, a window, or a mirror.

On the sixth day of Christmas my true love gave to me six geese a-laying.

Since eggs symbolize new life, the geese stand for the six days of creation described in Genesis.

here's how...

1 Start with a purchased silver box with a lid. From a crafts store or florist's supply shop, buy a miniature vine nest, a beaded egg, and goose feathers. Or make a beaded egg by gluing a strand of amber glass beads around a plastic foam egg.

2 Glue the vine nest to the lid, then glue the beaded egg in the nest. Tuck goose feathers around the egg, then trim the number label to the desired size and glue it in the nest. Glue ribbon around box, hiding the ends under the nest.

activities

Decorate a dozen or more raw eggs with nontoxic markers or crayons. Write special messages on them, draw faces, or just add squiggles and dots. Place them back in the egg cartons for later use. It will make cooking lots more fun for the next few weeks.

On the seventh day of Christmas my true love gave to me seven swans a-swimming.

Graceful swans symbolize the seven gifts of grace of the Holy Spirit, as listed in the twelfth book of Romans.

here's how...

1 To make a swan container, enlarge the patterns *at right* on a copier 190 percent and cut them out. On a piece of #120 Bristol Plate cardboard or other lightweight cardboard (from an art supply store), trace two body pieces, two wings, and one bottom piece. Cut out the shapes. (Note: The swan heads and necks must be the exact same size, so cut out both pieces simultaneously.) Trim the tail with scallop-cut and pinking shears and the wings with pinking shears.

2 Using a crafts knife, lightly score the bottom side of the bottom piece along the flaps (the broken lines on the pattern). Turn the piece over and score the center. Fold along the scored lines; set aside. Cut the feathers into the wings and curl them.

3 Glue the wings to the body pieces. Glue black seed beads in place for eyes

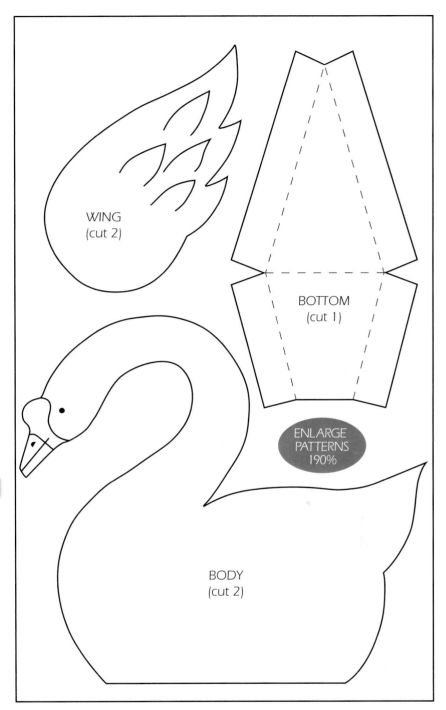

WING
(cut 2)

BOTTOM
(cut 1)

ENLARGE PATTERNS 190%

BODY
(cut 2)

and color the beak with black and orange markers. Glue the bodies together at the head and neck and along the front of the breast. Insert the bottom piece and glue the flaps to the swan pieces. Cut a slit in the beak for the label.

4 Twist several strands of wired berries into a 6-inch garland. Wire the ends to form a wreath. Slip the wreath over the swan's head. Cut the number label into a ¾×6-inch strip; clip the ends and slide into the slit in the beak.

activities

Take the family swimming at an indoor pool at your fitness center, or check into a hotel for the day and use its pool.

across the bridge of the shoe and add ribbon roses as shown.

2 For the number label, cut around the number with scallop-edge scissors and glue it to the side of the shoe. Wrap the gift in tissue paper and slip it into the shoe.

activities

Have family members teach each other new dances. Parents can get out the oldies and do the dances that were hot when they were young; teens can share the newest crazes; and younger ones can show off their new ballet or tumbling moves. End the night with everyone doing the Hokey Pokey, Bunny Hop, or a conga line.

On the eighth day of Christmas my true love gave to me eight maids a-milking.

Milkmaids, as humble servants, are supposed to represent the Beatitudes listed in Matthew.

here's how...

1 Look for a 5-inch diameter aluminum pail (available at crafts stores and florist's supply shops) for the gift container. Wire five small silver balls into a cluster and attach it to one handle of the pail. Make a bow from ribbon scraps and cording, then wire the bow to the pail handle over the ball cluster.

2 Trim the number label to fit a metal-rimmed package label (from a stationery store) and glue it in place. Attach the label to the pail with a short length of silver

bead chain (you can find this at hardware stores). Cut a 13-inch-square of fabric to wrap the gift, and tuck it inside the pail.

activities

Enjoy the end result of all that milking with the season's favorite dairy treats—gourmet hot chocolate or some decadent ice cream.

On the ninth day of Christmas my true love gave to me nine ladies dancing.

The nine ladies symbolize the fruits of the Spirit as listed in Galatians.

here's how...

1 Look for a wire mesh ballet slipper at a crafts store or a florist's supply shop. Spray the shoe with metallic chrome paint and let it dry. Glue a scrap of ribbon

---

On the tenth day of Christmas my true love gave to me 10 lords a-leaping.

In the Middle Ages, lords could, to some extent, define the law within their own lands. So the 10 lords are the Ten Commandments.

here's how...

1 For a more playful interpretation of this verse, decorate a small oval cardboard box with frog stickers. You'll find all of the supplies at a crafts store.

2 Glue a pink plastic jewel to the center of the box lid; slip small silver beads onto a length of thread with a beading needle to make a chain that fits around the jewel. Cover the sides of the box and lid with ribbon and trim the edge of the lid with silver cord.

activities

Have a family game day. Along with jumping, running, and relay races, include nontraditional "sports" like Frisbee tossing, pillow throwing, thumb wrestling, whistling, or finger snapping. Be sure every family member has one category he or she is sure to win. The sillier the categories are, the better.

On the eleventh day of Christmas my true love gave to me 11 *pipers piping.*

The pipers are the eleven disciples who remained faithful.

here's how...

For this gift wrap, look through clip-art books for an image of a piper, or use a scrap of toile. To add color, you can have the image enlarged and copied in red onto green paper at a copy center. Cover the box as directed under General Box Wrapping Instructions (page 48) and tie with satin ribbon. Trim the number label to the desired size and glue in place.

activities

Decorate a cake or cookies with piped frosting. To save time and make it easy, use canned frosting and a plain purchased cake or cookies. If you don't have a pastry bag and tips, look for frosting in a tube; it comes in different colors with plastic screw-on tips.

On the twelfth day of Christmas my true love gave to me 12 drummers drumming.

Drummers establish the rhythm for marching. They symbolize the 12 doctrines listed in the Apostles' Creed, an ancient summary of Christian beliefs.

here's how...

1 Start with a frosting can or other round can with a lid. Cut gold foil cardboard to the height and circumference of the can, adding ½ inch at one end for overlap. Glue the cardboard around the can. Trace the lid onto brown paper and cut it out, adding ¼ inch all around. Glue the paper to the lid, then clip the excess to the lid edge; fold it over the sides of the lid and glue.

2 Glue trims around the can and lid edge as desired. Place the lid on the can. Glue metallic gold braid to the drum for the strap and cover the raw ends with gold buttons. Cut two chopsticks or wooden skewers to 5 inches and glue them to the top of the drum. Trim the number label to the desired size; clip the ends in points and glue in place.

activities

Form an instant kitchen band with oatmeal boxes and cooking pans for drums, empty bottles for wind instruments, pan lids for cymbals, jars half-filled with dried beans or unpopped popcorn (for shaking), and glassware for bells or xylophones.

purchased evergreen wreath
raffia
hot-glue gun and glue sticks
2 small green apples
old garden trowel
From a florist's supply shop:
  fresh or dried artemisia
  Chinese tallow-tree berries
  preserved green oak leaves
  fresh rosemary
  medium-gauge florist's wire
From a garden shop:
  leftover paperwhite narcissus
    bulb
  3 miniature flowerpots

Give a garden-style theme to your outdoor decorations by incorporating hand tools, terra-cotta pots, and watering cans into wreaths, arrangements, and swags.

winter welcome

54

Garden Wreath

❧Give a plain fresh wreath a garden-grown personality by using what you can find in your own tool shed—an old or new trowel, small terra-cotta pots, and a narcissus bulb that's already finished blooming are all you need to create a wreath with character. Use silvery gray and white herbs and berries for a snow-kissed look.

here's how...

1 Cut the artemisia stems into pieces that are slightly shorter than the longest evergreen branches in the wreath. Apply hot glue to the bottom portion of the artemisia stems and insert them into the evergreens. The stems should point in the same direction so the artemisia leads the eye clockwise around the wreath.

2 Glue bunches of Chinese tallow-tree berries (also called popcorn berries) into the wreath in the same way. Add preserved oak leaves and fresh rosemary for contrasting textures.

3 Use florist's wire to attach the trowel to one side of the wreath. Wire the narcissus bulb at an angle above the trowel, and cover the wire with a raffia bow.

4 Wire the miniature flowerpots to the opposite half of the wreath. Wedge small green apples into two of the pots. If you use a pot with no hole, you can drill one using a masonry bit at slow speed.

56

Wheelbarrow Arrangement

Fill a wheelbarrow or wooden garden wagon with greenery, pinecones, and pots of fruit for a festive display in your yard or on your porch. Lay long branches of evergreens in the wheelbarrow so they spill over the front edge and extend out from the back. If possible, use several kinds of greenery so you'll have a variety of textures and shades of green. Here the homeowner combined western cedar, Douglas fir, red huckleberry, white pine, and variegated privet. Anchor the branches with terra-cotta pots nestled into the greenery, and fill the pots with apples or other fruits. Add large sugar pinecones, bundles of sticks or birch twigs, and an old watering can filled with evergreens for a focal point.

Pinecone Swag

❧Pinecones and terra-cotta "bells" make a graceful, country-style swag for your porch or a lamppost.

here's how...

1 Using a ⁵⁄₆₄-inch drill bit, drill a hole in the base of each sugar pinecone. Insert one end of a 4-inch piece of wire into the hole, and secure it with a drop of hot glue. Twist the other end of the wire around itself to make a loop.

2 Cut the rope into 5-foot lengths, one for each cone. Thread one length of rope through the wire loop on each cone.

3 Cut the remaining rope into three pieces of varying lengths. Knot one end of each piece and thread the remaining end through the hole in the bottom of each terra-cotta pot.

4 Gather all the ropes in your hand and adjust them so the cones and pots hang at different lengths. Tie the ropes in a knot.

5 Wire evergreens to the ropes along the length of the swag.

58

Birdhouse Swag

Turn a decorative birdhouse into the centerpiece of a holiday swag. For accents use—what else?—seed-covered plastic foam balls.

here's how...

1 Center the birdhouse on the 1×3 and nail it to the board. (If possible, open the birdhouse lid and nail from the inside of the house into the board.)

Use pan-melt hotmelt adhesive to glue foam blocks to the 1×3 above and below the birdhouse. To reinforce the glue, wrap florist's tape around the blocks and board as shown.

To make the seed balls, push a wooden skewer into each plastic foam ball. Apply a thick coat of crafts glue to the ball and roll it in your choice of birdseed, other seeds (such as poppy seeds, fennel, mustard seeds, or grass seed), or beans. (Alternatively, you can purchase seed-covered balls at florist's supply shops or crafts stores and attach them to florist's picks.) Let the glue dry, then fill any empty spaces with additional seeds.

4 With a knife, sharpen the stem end of each branch of pine, fir, or juniper, and push the stems into the plastic foam blocks. Use longer pieces of greenery in the bottom block for a visually heavier base to balance the birdhouse. Tuck a few stems just below the birdhouse to extend horizontally, forming a shelf. Insert the largest seed ball under the birdhouse and add a small and medium one as shown. Insert three medium and small balls above the birdhouse.

59

◀ Bundle eight to 10 dripless candles and tie them together tightly with a bow. (Choose candles with flat, not shaped, bottoms.) Stand them in a footed hurricane vase. Keep the bow well away from the flames and never leave burning candles unattended.

In a Twinkling:
Candles

▲ For an autumn centerpiece, use a hot-glue gun to attach preserved or artificial autumn leaves to a plain hurricane lamp. The candlelight will glow warmly through the leaves.

◀ For a quick, frosted effect, use white acrylic crafts paint to decorate a hurricane lamp. Make swirls, dots, and swags in a free-form design for a lighthearted, handcrafted look. Place a white pillar candle inside, and rest both candle and lamp on a plain white dish to catch any candle drips. Embellish votives in clear glass containers with paint to give purchased candles a personal touch too.

For a quick holiday candleholder, spray a small terra-cotta pot silver, then fill it with floral foam. Push a votive candle into the floral foam to anchor it, then add sprigs of fresh holly around the base of the candle (and well away from the flames).

For a mantel or centerpiece decoration with a playful feeling, glue gumdrops, watermelon-slice candies, and peppermints to a hurricane lamp, using a hot-glue gun.

Religious candles, available at grocery stores, come in tall, clear glass containers. For a simple holiday accent, wrap the containers with handcrafted paper from an art supply store and tie with twine.

GATHERI

What's the secret to a successful party? A carefully chosen guest list is key. Think about people who will enjoy each other's company and will have some common ground for conversation. Interesting food helps, too, but that doesn't mean you have to spend hours in the kitchen. The simplest fare imaginable—fruit, cheese, bread, and wine—can be a gastronomic delight and requires little more than a stop at the grocery store. The most important ingredient, however, is your own enthusiasm. If you're focused on making your friends feel welcome, everything else falls into place. Whether you offer a four-course meal you've prepared yourself, or order take-out and serve it on your best china, make sure you give yourself time to enjoy your guests.

NGtogether

63

Poppy Seed Flats
(see recipe, page 71)

64

There are few ways of entertaining that are simpler or more classic than a wine-and-cheese party. Just choose and present cheeses with a few accompaniments and open the wine.

cheese, *please*

Whether you're hosting a wine-and-cheese-tasting party for the holidays or serving a French-style after-dinner cheese course any time of year, it's important to choose the cheeses carefully. You'll want variety in terms of each cheese's texture, flavor, and milk source (the animal that contributed the milk to make it). For instance, although Stilton, Roquefort, and Maytag Blue come from different milk sources and have different texture and flavor qualities, they are all blue-veined cheeses—so you'll probably want to serve just one of them.

If you're going to serve a hard, piquant (sharp-tasting) cheese made from sheep's milk, be sure you serve a softer, sweeter—even spreadable—cow's milk cheese to complement it. In making your selections, consider not only the classic, centuries-old European cheeses, such as Italian Parmigiano-Reggiano and Dutch Gouda, but also some of the up-and-coming artisanal cheeses being made regionally in this country—many of which are flavored with herbs, whole black peppercorns, chiles, or wild mushrooms. One such cheese is a full-bodied, aged, dry Monterey Jack from California.

Generally, you'll want to serve between three and five cheeses for a good sampling. Check your grocery or local gourmet delicatessen to see what is available. For starters, mix and match from the chart above. The cheeses are listed by similar textures, with firm-textured cheeses at the beginning of the list, and the creamy, soft, and spreadable ones at the end.

cheese	origin	milk source	texture	flavor
Manchego	Spain	Sheep	Firm	Mellow
Scamorza	Italy	Cow	Firm	Mildly smoky
Gruyère	Switzerland, France	Cow	Firm	Mild, nutty
Aged cheddar	U.S., England	Cow	Firm, crumbly	Sharp
Parmigiano-Reggiano	Italy	Cow	Hard	Nutty, tangy
Pecorino Romano	Italy	Sheep	Hard	Sharp, piquant
Dry Monterey Jack	California	Cow	Hard	Full-bodied, tangy
Aged Gouda (18 to 24 months)	Holland	Cow	Hard	Nutty, caramel
Stilton	England	Cow	Soft; slightly crumbly	Slightly assertive
Roquefort	France	Sheep	Creamy, rich	Assertive, slightly salty
Maytag Blue	Iowa	Cow	Soft; crumbly	Tangy, peppery
Mascarpone	Italy	Cow	Spreadable	Mild, sweet
Fresh goat cheese	France, U.S.	Goat	Spreadable	Earthy, mild
Brie	France, U.S.	Cow	Creamy	Buttery, slightly tangy
Fresh mozzarella	Italy, U.S.	Cow or buffalo	Soft	Mild, sweet

65

Fresh mozzarella

Gruyère

Scamorza

Aged Gouda

Mascarpone

Aged cheddar

Dry Monterey Jack

wine and cheese

There are several reasons wine and cheese seem to get along so genially. First and foremost, they both rely on living organisms for their very existence—not to mention for their unique flavors. Wines use yeast and cheeses use bacterial cultures. Their denomination or *terroir*—where they were made—also has tremendous influence on the characteristics of both wine and cheese.

For cheese, a key to flavor may be what the animal whose milk was used to make it grazed on. For wine, the keys may be the soil and the amount of sunshine and rain the grapes got as they were growing. Wine and cheese are also both greatly influenced by centuries— even thousands of years—of techniques, some of which haven't changed much since the first time they were used. Both are aged to varying degrees, ranging from months to years. Aging both wine and cheese contributes to their characters and the complexity of their flavors, texture (cheese), and body (wine).

Perhaps most importantly, though, their compatibility on the palate is a natural: The saltiness of cheese calls for something to sip, and the alcohol in the wine cuts the richness of the cheese on the palate (so you can eat even more cheese!).

Some say a guideline for pairing wines with cheeses is that aged cheeses taste best with old wine, fresher cheeses with younger wines. Since aging intensifies the flavor and complexity of both wine and cheese, you want those qualities of each to be about equal; you don't want your wine to overpower your cheese or vice versa. Another simple guideline to keep in mind is that cheeses and wines from the same regions generally go well together. You don't have to follow those rules exclusively (or even the suggestions made in the box at left), but the chart is a starting place for making a good marriage.

cheese	wine
Manchego	Sherry (fino), Rioja, Spanish sparkling whites (cava)
Scamorza	Pinot Grigio, Orvieto
Gruyère	Riesling, Sauvignon Blanc, Fumé Blanc, Gewürztraminer
Aged cheddar	Syrah (Shiraz), Petite Sirah, Zinfandel
Parmigiano-Reggiano	Chianti Classico, Merlot
Pecorino Romano	Barolo, Gattinara, Barbaresco
Dry Monterey Jack	Dry Riesling, Gewürztraminer, Petite Sirah
Aged Gouda	Pinot Noir, Zinfandel
Stilton	Port, Pinot Noir, good-quality Sauternes
Roquefort	French red Burgundy, Côtes du Rhône, Vouvray
Maytag Blue	Cabernet Sauvignon, Syrah (Shiraz)
Mascarpone	Frascati, Italian Soave
Fresh goat cheese	Beaujolais, dry sparkling wine, Champagne
Brie	Côtes du Rhône, Pouilly-Fuissé, Bordeaux
Fresh mozzarella	Bardolino, Valpolicella

fruit and cheese

Good accompaniments for cheeses include breads, crackers, nuts, and of course, fresh and dried fruits. You almost can't go wrong pairing any kind of fruit with any kind of cheese, but consider the combinations listed below.

cheese	fruit
Manchego	Avocado, grapefruit sections, mango
Scamorza	Melon, nectarines
Gruyère	Apples, plums
Aged cheddar	Apples
Parmigiano-Reggiano	Fresh figs, melon
Pecorino Romano	Fresh or dried figs, melon
Dry Monterey Jack	Persimmons, plums
Aged Gouda	Fresh or dried apricots
Stilton	Pears, apples
Roquefort	Prunes, ripe plums
Maytag Blue	Dried cranberries or dried cherries
Mascarpone	Fresh berries, fresh cherries
Fresh goat cheese	Fresh or dried figs, dates, plums
Brie	Red or green grapes
Fresh mozzarella	Orange sections (such as ruby-fleshed blood oranges), peaches

67

staging a wine-and-cheese party

Within the wine-and-cheese genre, there are several ways to go. You might decide to serve only several kinds of sherry, along with an array of Spanish cheeses—or several sparkling wines and Champagne with an assortment of French cheeses. It's nice, too, to offer guests a selection of cheeses (hard, creamy, tangy, mild) to sample, matched with complementary wines (red, white, and sparkling).

You'll want to serve between three and five cheeses, providing a variety of textures, tastes, and origins. Bring them out of the refrigerator one hour before you plan on serving them for maximum flavor—but unwrap them right before serving to prevent them from drying out. Arrange them on a large platter with an assortment of fresh and dried fruits (or arrange those separately). Place a selection of breads and crackers in a linen-lined basket. Be sure to have a variety of sweeter, whole-grain breads and crackers as well as crusty, chewy French-style breads and thin, crisp, lavosh-style crackers.

For a traditional and elegant presentation, you might try arranging the cheeses atop cheese leaves—paper cutouts that look like leaves—which are available where fine cheeses are sold. (Leaves are associated with cheese because many types—such as the Spanish cheese, Cabrales, or Banon, a goat cheese from France—are aged wrapped in various sorts of leaves, which impart their flavor to the rind.) Provide a cheese plane (a kind of slicer that makes thin, melt-in-your-mouth pieces) for harder cheeses and a knife or spreader for each softer cheese. Each cheese needs its own serving utensil to prevent mixing flavors.

You can lay everything out all at once on the buffet or dining room table, or you can follow the guidelines used at formal dinners and bring wines and cheeses on in stages: a dry wine before a sweet one, a white wine before a red, a young wine before an aged wine.

Most people don't have the perfectly appropriate wine glass for each kind of wine, but if you are serving a sparkling wine, be sure to have flutes along with plenty of clean wine glasses for tasting—at least two for each guest, if possible. Be sure to provide your guests with lots of napkins and small dessert or luncheon plates to carry their nibbles as they mingle and make merry.

Roasted Pepper Focaccia

You can substitute roasted peppers that come in a jar. Just be sure to drain them well before cutting into thin strips.

- 3¼ to 3¾ cups bread flour or all-purpose flour
- 1 package active dry yeast
- 2 tablespoons snipped fresh rosemary
- 1 teaspoon salt
- ⅛ teaspoon baking soda
- 1¼ cups warm water (120° to 130°)
- 2 tablespoons olive oil
- ¼ cup finely shredded aged provolone cheese (1 ounce)
- 2 red and/or yellow sweet peppers
- 4 teaspoons olive oil
- ¼ teaspoon freshly ground pepper
- ¼ cup pine nuts
- ½ cup finely shredded aged provolone cheese (2 ounces)

Combine 1¼ cups of the flour, the yeast, rosemary, salt, and baking soda in a large mixing bowl. Add water and the 2 tablespoons oil. Beat with electric mixer on low to medium speed for 30 seconds, scraping bowl. Beat on high speed 3 minutes. Using a spoon, stir in the ¼ cup cheese and as much remaining flour as you can.

Turn dough out onto a lightly floured surface. Knead in enough remaining flour to make a stiff dough that is smooth and elastic (8 to 10 minutes). Shape dough into a ball. Place in a lightly greased bowl; turn once to grease surface. Cover and let rise in a warm place until double (about 1 hour).

Meanwhile, to roast sweet peppers, quarter the peppers; remove and discard stems, seeds, and membranes. Place pepper quarters, cut sides down, on a baking sheet lined with foil. Bake in a 425° oven for 20 to 25 minutes or until pepper skins are blistered and dark. Remove from oven; reduce oven temperature to 375°. Immediately wrap peppers in the foil. Let stand about 30 minutes to steam so skins peel away easily. Remove and discard skin from peppers. Cut peppers into thin strips.

Grease 2 baking sheets. Punch down dough. Turn out onto a lightly floured surface. Divide in half. Shape each half into a ball and place on a prepared baking sheet. Cover and let rest for 10 minutes. Using your hands, flatten each ball to about 12 inches in diameter. Cover and let rise until nearly double (about 20 minutes). With flour-dusted fingers, press fingers into dough making ½-inch-deep indentations. Repeat to cover dough, spacing indentations 1 to 2 inches apart.

Brush dough with the 4 teaspoons oil. Sprinkle with ground pepper. Top with pepper strips, pine nuts, and the ½ cup cheese. Bake in a 375° oven about 20 minutes or until golden. Transfer to wire racks. Cool completely. Tear or cut into wedges. Makes 16 servings.

Nutrition facts per serving: 161 cal., 6 g total fat (2 g sat. fat), 4 mg chol., 191 mg sodium, 21 g carbo., 1 g fiber, 6 g pro. **Daily values:** 8% vit. A, 26% vit. C, 3% calcium, 9% iron

68

Manchego

Parmigiano-Reggiano

Pecorino Romano

Maytag Blue

Fresh goat cheese

Roquefort

Brie

69

Gorgonzola-Onion Tart

Mini Gruyère Puffs

70

Gorgonzola-Onion Tart

✳

The sweetness of caramelized onions spiked with a little brown sugar is a nice complement to the rich, pungent taste of Gorgonzola, blue, or feta cheese in this appetizer served in wedges.

½ of a 15-ounce package folded refrigerated unbaked piecrust (1 crust)
2 tablespoons butter or margarine
1 tablespoon brown sugar
1 teaspoon vinegar
2 medium onions, quartered lengthwise and thinly sliced (about 1⅓ cups)
4 ounces Gorgonzola, blue, or feta cheese, crumbled (1 cup)

2 eggs
1 teaspoon dried chervil or marjoram, crushed
¼ teaspoon pepper
⅓ cup milk, half-and-half, or light cream
3 tablespoons dry white wine or chicken broth
2 tablespoons snipped fresh parsley
1 beaten egg yolk
Green onions (optional)

Roll piecrust from center to edges on a lightly floured surface forming a circle about 12 inches in diameter. Ease pastry into a 9-inch tart pan with a removable bottom, pressing dough up into fluted sides of tart pan. Trim edges, reserving scraps. Do not prick pastry. Line pastry with a double thickness of foil. Bake in a 450° oven for 8 minutes. Remove foil. Bake 4 minutes more or until crust is dry and set. Reduce oven temperature to 375°.

For filling, melt butter in a medium skillet; stir in brown sugar and vinegar. Add onions. Cook, uncovered, over medium-low heat for 10 to 12 minutes or until onions are tender and light brown, stirring occasionally.

Beat cheese, eggs, chervil or marjoram, and pepper in a mixing bowl with an electric mixer on low speed until combined (cheese will still be lumpy). By hand, stir in onion mixture, milk, wine, and parsley. Ladle filling evenly into baked tart shell.

Bake tart in a 375° oven about 20 minutes or until a knife inserted near center of filling comes out clean and pastry is golden. Cool 15 minutes in pan on a wire rack.

Meanwhile, roll out piecrust scraps to ⅛ inch thickness; cut into decorative shapes with small cutters. Place on ungreased baking sheet. Brush lightly with a mixture of egg yolk and 1 teaspoon *water*. Bake cutouts in 375° oven for 6 to 7 minutes or until golden. Carefully remove sides of tart pan. Decorate top with baked cutouts and add green onion curls, if desired. Cut tart into wedges. Serve while warm. Makes 12 appetizers.

Nutrition facts per appetizer: 163 cal., 11 g total fat (3 g sat. fat), 71 mg chol., 237 mg sodium, 11 g carbo., 0 g fiber, 4 g pro. **Daily values:** 8% vit. A, 2% vit. C, 5% calcium, 2% iron

Poppy Seed Flats

See photo, page 64.

- 1¾ cups all-purpose flour
- ¾ cup yellow cornmeal
- 2 tablespoons dried minced onion
- 1 tablespoon sugar
- 1½ teaspoons poppy seed
- ½ teaspoon baking soda
- ½ teaspoon salt
- 3 tablespoons butter
- ¾ cup milk
- 1 egg white
- 1 tablespoon poppy seed

Well grease a baking sheet or line with parchment paper; set aside. Stir together flour, cornmeal, onion, sugar, the 1½ teaspoons poppy seed, baking soda, and salt in a medium mixing bowl. Using a pastry blender, cut in butter until mixture resembles coarse crumbs. Make a well in center of flour mixture. Add milk. Using a fork, stir until dough can be gathered into a ball.

Turn dough out onto a lightly floured surface. Knead for 8 to 10 strokes or until dough is almost smooth. Divide into 3 portions. Roll each portion to a 12×9-inch rectangle on a lightly floured surface. Using a fork, prick rectangles well. Using a pastry wheel, cut each into twelve 4½×2-inch rectangles. Place 1 inch apart on baking sheet.

Combine egg white and 1 tablespoon *water*; lightly brush over rectangles. Sprinkle with 1 tablespoon poppy seed.

Bake in a 375° oven for 10 to 12 minutes or until browned and crisp. Transfer to wire racks to cool. Store in an airtight container for up to 3 days. Serve with sliced cheeses, if desired. Makes 36 crackers.

Nutrition facts per cracker: 46 cal., 1 g total fat (1 g sat. fat), 3 mg chol., 65 mg sodium, 7 g carbo., 1 g fiber, 1 g pro. **Daily values:** 1% vit. A, 0% vit. C, 1% calcium, 2% iron

Mini Gruyère Puffs

The French call these little cheese-flavored pastries gougére and they're a classic hors d'oeuvre. Crisp on the outside and soft and custardy on the inside, they're terrific hot out of the oven with chilled white wine or champagne.

- ½ cup water
- ¼ cup butter
- ½ teaspoon dried basil, crushed
- ¼ teaspoon garlic salt
  Dash ground red pepper
- ½ cup all-purpose flour
- 2 eggs
- ½ cup shredded Gruyère or Swiss cheese (2 ounces)
- 2 tablespoons grated Parmesan cheese

Combine water and butter in a small saucepan. Add basil, garlic salt, and red pepper. Bring to boiling over medium heat, stirring to melt butter. Add flour all at once, stirring vigorously. Cook and stir until mixture forms a ball that doesn't separate. Remove from heat. Cool 5 minutes.

Grease a baking sheet. Add eggs, one at a time, to saucepan, beating with a spoon after each addition until smooth. Stir in Gruyère cheese. Drop mounds of dough by rounded teaspoons, about 2 inches apart, on a prepared baking sheet. Sprinkle with Parmesan cheese.

Bake in a 450° oven for 10 minutes. Reduce oven temperature to 375° and bake 10 to 12 minutes more or until puffed and golden. Turn off oven. Let puffs remain in oven for 3 minutes. Serve hot. Makes about 20 appetizers.

Nutrition facts per appetizer: 53 cal., 4 g total fat (2 g sat. fat), 31 mg chol., 76 mg sodium, 2 g carbo., 0 g fiber, 2 g pro. **Daily values:** 4% vit. A, 0% vit. C, 3% calcium, 1% iron

71

Prime Rib au Poivre
(see recipe, page 79)

72

Pea Pods and Onions with Dill Butter
(see recipe, page 78)

An elegant, sit-down dinner with a multi-course menu is not a gastronomic relic—and here's proof: a soup-to-nuts holiday menu featuring wild mushroom soup, a stunning prime rib roast, and wild rice stuffed into mini squash.

the pleasures *of the* table

table setting tips

As much as we may enjoy the trend toward casual entertaining, a festive occasion such as Christmas or New Year's calls for a more formal (not stuffy!) sit-down dinner.

Once you've got your wonderful menu planned, you want a table setting that is equally lovely to complement the great food. A sit-down dinner is a nice way to serve a group of perhaps 12 guests at the most. Don't fret about whether your dining table can accommodate that many. If not, set up an extra table in the living room. Once you've got it covered in pretty linens and set with sparkling dishes and a centerpiece, no one will be the wiser that it's the card table you brought up from the basement.

The foundation of the table, of course, is the linens. For a formal dinner, consider a lace or crisp white linen tablecloth and napkins. Or, dress the table in a beautiful antique embroidered sheet or quilt topped with a washable, coordinating cloth.

As a guideline, use the place setting arrangement sketched below. Of course, no table is complete without a lovely centerpiece (see pages 86–99 for ideas).

menu *for* twelve

Wild Mushroom Soup

———

Walnut Rolls - Butter

✱

Prime Rib au Poivre

———

Pea Pods and Onions
with Dill Butter

———

Wild Rice-Stuffed Squash

———

Peach-Fig Relish

———

Fennel and Sweet
Pepper Salad

✱

Pumpkin-Pecan Cheesecake

———

Choice of Beverages

74

Walnut Rolls
(see recipe, page 79)

Wild Mushroom Soup

Wild Mushroom Soup

½ cup chicken broth
1 ounce dried porcini or other
   dried wild mushrooms
¼ cup dry Madeira, dry sherry, or
   chicken broth
½ cup butter
¼ cup chopped onion
1 pound fresh button
   mushrooms, sliced
   (about 6 cups)
4 ounces shiitake mushrooms,
   stems removed and
   discarded, and sliced (about
   1½ cups)
⅔ cup all-purpose flour
8 cups chicken broth
½ teaspoon cracked black pepper
1½ cups buttermilk

Bring the ½ cup broth to boiling in a small saucepan; add dried mushrooms and wine to boiling broth. Remove from heat. Let stand, covered, 20 minutes. Drain and discard excess liquid. Coarsely chop mushrooms; set aside.

Melt butter in a 4-quart Dutch oven over medium heat. Add onion; cook and stir for 2 to 3 minutes or until tender. Stir in fresh and dried mushrooms; cook 3 to 4 minutes more or until mushrooms are tender and most of the liquid has evaporated. Stir in the flour.

Add the 8 cups broth and the pepper. Bring to boiling; reduce heat. Simmer, uncovered, 30 minutes more, stirring occasionally.* Stir in buttermilk and heat through, but do not boil. If desired, garnish individual servings with green onion tops. Makes 12 servings.

MAKE-AHEAD TIP: Prepare soup through the *. Cover and refrigerate up to 24 hours. To serve, stir in buttermilk and heat through.

Nutrition facts per serving: 152 cal., 9 g total fat (5 g sat. fat), 22 mg chol., 644 mg sodium, 11 g carbo., 1 g fiber, 6 g pro. **Daily values:** 7% vit. A, 4% vit. C, 4% calcium, 10% iron

MENU TIMETABLE

several days ahead:
■ Have plenty of ice on hand; chill sparkling water, other beverages, and wine, if desired.
■ Iron the tablecloth and napkins.
■ Prepare Walnut Rolls; wrap tightly and freeze.
■ Prepare, cover, and refrigerate the Peach-Fig Relish.
■ Select and set out serving containers to be used.

1 day ahead:
■ Prepare Wild Mushroom Soup through the simmering step. Cover and refrigerate.
■ Prepare rice filling and cook the mini squash for Wild Rice-Stuffed Squash. Cover and refrigerate in separate containers.
■ Prepare dressing for Fennel and Sweet Pepper Salad. Cover and refrigerate.
■ Prepare the Pumpkin-Pecan Cheesecake; cover tightly and refrigerate. Toast pecans for the cheesecake garnish; set aside.
■ Cut butter sticks into pats and place in serving bowl; cover and refrigerate.

4 hours ahead:
■ Set out the plates, flatware, serving pieces, and glassware.
■ Arrange the centerpiece, candles, and other table decorations.
■ Prepare vegetables for the Fennel and Sweet Pepper Salad and place ingredients in large bowls or plastic bags; cover and refrigerate.

3½ hours ahead:
■ Start preparing Prime Rib au Poivre and place in oven (exact time depends on desired doneness of meat). Add squash to oven when meat is 20 to 25 degrees from desired doneness.
■ Remove rolls from freezer to thaw.

1 hour ahead:
■ Prepare the strawberry garnish for the Pumpkin-Pecan Cheesecake; cover and refrigerate.
■ Remove rice filling and squash from the refrigerator and let stand at room temperature for 30 minutes. Then spoon the filling into the squash. Add squash to oven with the beef roast and bake about 25 minutes or until hot.

30 minutes ahead:
■ Remove salad dressing from refrigerator and let the dressing stand at room temperature.
■ Spoon Peach-Fig Relish into a serving dish and add a sprig of mint and some cranberries for the garnish.
■ Stir buttermilk into the Wild Mushroom Soup and heat through.
■ Prepare Pea Pods and Onions with Dill Butter.
■ Start preparations for the coffee and/or tea.

just before serving:
■ Arrange Walnut Rolls in a napkin-lined basket.
■ Pour any chilled beverages.
■ Light the candles.
■ Ladle soup into soup plates or bowls.
■ Shake dressing. Drizzle dressing over salad in bowls. If desired, toss salad lightly to coat with dressing.
■ Place squash on serving platter and add sage leaf and kumquat garnish.
■ Place roast on platter and arrange some of the pea pod mixture around the beef roast; transfer the rest of the vegetables to a serving bowl.
■ Beat the whipping cream. Cut cheesecake into wedges and garnish top of cheesecake with whipped cream and toasted pecans. If desired, trim individual servings with fresh strawberries or other fresh fruit.
■ Pour beverages to go with dessert.

75

Wild Rice-Stuffed Squash

To preserve the pretty presentation of these individual servings of whole stuffed squash, look for small squash varieties such as those suggested. Each squash should weigh only about 6 ounces.

2 14½-ounce cans reduced-sodium chicken broth
1 teaspoon dried thyme, crushed
⅔ cup uncooked wild rice, rinsed
3 medium leeks, green parts removed, ends trimmed, and chopped (1 cup)
⅔ cup uncooked long grain rice
12 small winter squash (such as acorn, Sweet Dumpling, or Golden Nugget), each about 3½ to 4 inches in diameter
¼ cup butter or margarine, cut up
½ cup dried cranberries or dried currants
½ cup dried apricots, snipped
¼ teaspoon salt
¼ teaspoon pepper
   Fresh sage leaves (optional)
   Fresh kumquats (optional)

Bring chicken broth and thyme to boiling in a large saucepan. Add uncooked wild rice; reduce heat. Cook, covered, for 30 minutes. Add leeks and uncooked long grain rice. Cover and simmer 15 minutes more or until rice is tender. Let stand, covered, 5 minutes. Drain excess liquid, if necessary.

Meanwhile, wash squash; cut off and discard the top one-third from the stem end of each. Scrape out seeds with a spoon. Place squash, cut sides down, in a 15×10×1-inch baking pan. Bake in a 350° oven for 50 minutes or until tender. Remove and set aside.

Stir butter, dried cranberries, dried apricots, salt, and pepper into rice mixture until butter melts.

Mound stuffing into squash. Return to baking pan. Cover with foil. Bake in a 350° oven for 20 to 25 minutes or

until heated through. Garnish with sage leaves and kumquats, if desired. Makes 12 side-dish servings.

MAKE-AHEAD TIP: Prepare rice filling and cook the squash until tender; cover and refrigerate up to 24 hours. To serve, let squash and rice mixture stand at room temperature 30 minutes. Fill and bake as directed until heated through.

Nutrition facts per serving: 205 cal., 5 g total fat (2 g sat. fat), 10 mg chol., 287 mg sodium, 40 g carbo., 5 g fiber, 5 g pro. **Daily values:** 107% vit. A, 38% vit. C, 6% calcium, 14% iron

Peach-Fig Relish

What's a big holiday meal without a great relish like this one—a spiced, aromatic mix of canned and dried fruits.

1 29-ounce can peach slices
1 5½-ounce can peach nectar
¼ teaspoon finely shredded lemon peel
2 tablespoons lemon juice
¾ teaspoon ground cardamom
1 12-ounce package dried light-colored figs, snipped (1½ cups)
2 tablespoons brandy or orange juice
   Cranberries (optional)
   Fresh mint sprigs (optional)

Drain peaches, reserving ½ cup syrup. Coarsely chop peaches. Heat peaches, reserved syrup, peach nectar, lemon peel, lemon juice, and cardamom in a medium saucepan until boiling. Boil gently, uncovered, for 5 minutes.

Stir in figs and brandy or orange juice. Cook and stir 2 minutes more or until desired consistency. Remove from heat; cool. Place in a bowl; cover with plastic wrap. Refrigerate at least 2 hours before serving. Garnish with cranberries and fresh mint sprigs, if desired. Makes 4 cups (12 servings).

MAKE-AHEAD TIP: Prepare relish. Cover and refrigerate up to 1 week.

Nutrition facts per serving: 133 cal., 0 g total fat (0 g sat. fat), 0 mg chol., 8 mg sodium, 33 g carbo., 3 g fiber, 1 g pro. **Daily values:** 2% vit. A, 6% vit. C, 3% calcium, 5% iron

Fennel and Sweet Pepper Salad

Many Italians serve slices of crisp, fresh fennel bulbs as a palate-refresher with their big Christmas feast. This holiday salad—made slightly sweet with balsamic vinegar—takes advantage of this anise-flavored vegetable at its seasonal peak. Use white balsamic vinegar if you want the fennel to stay white.

4 large fennel bulbs
4 large red sweet peppers
2 heads Bibb or Boston lettuce, torn (10 cups)
2 bunches watercress (2 cups leaves)
½ cup olive oil
⅓ cup balsamic vinegar
1 teaspoon fennel seed, crushed
½ teaspoon salt
¼ teaspoon pepper

Discard outer layers of fennel; halve and remove core. Slice fennel crosswise into thin strips (about 4¾ cups). Halve peppers lengthwise; remove seeds. Slice peppers crosswise into thin half-rings.

Combine fennel, sweet peppers, Bibb or Boston lettuce, and watercress in one very large (or two regular-size) salad bowl. Garnish with additional sweet pepper rings, if desired.

For dressing, combine olive oil, balsamic vinegar, fennel seed, salt, and pepper in a screw-top jar. Cover and shake well. Just before serving, drizzle dressing over salad and toss lightly to coat. Makes 12 servings.

Nutrition facts per serving: 108 cal., 9 g total fat (1 g sat. fat), 0 mg chol., 112 mg sodium, 6 g carbo., 10 g fiber, 1 g pro. **Daily values:** 33% vit. A, 94% vit. C, 3% calcium, 3% iron

Fennel and Sweet Pepper Salad

Peach-Fig Relish

Wild Rice-Stuffed Squash

77

Pumpkin-Pecan Cheesecake

remainder aside. Add pumpkin, the 1 egg, milk, cinnamon, ginger, and nutmeg to bowl. Beat on low speed just until combined. Pour pumpkin mixture into prepared springform pan. Top with cream cheese mixture. With a knife or narrow metal spatula, gently swirl through the layers to marble.

Place springform pan in a shallow baking pan. Bake in a 350° oven for 40 to 45 minutes or until center appears set when shaken. Cool on a wire rack for 15 minutes. Loosen crust from sides of pan. Cool 30 minutes more; remove sides of pan. Cool completely. Cover and chill at least 4 hours.

Before serving, beat whipping cream until stiff peaks form. Pipe or spoon into mounds atop cheesecake. Garnish with pecans and fresh strawberries, if desired. Makes 12 to 16 servings.

Nutrition facts per serving: 323 cal., 22 g total fat (13 g sat. fat), 132 mg chol., 195 mg sodium, 26 g carbo., 1 g fiber, 6 g pro. **Daily values:** 102% vit. A, 3% vit. C, 7% calcium, 9% iron

Pumpkin-Pecan Cheesecake

½ cup finely crushed graham crackers
¼ cup finely crushed gingersnaps
2 tablespoons finely chopped pecans
1 tablespoon all-purpose flour
1 tablespoon powdered sugar
2 tablespoons butter or margarine, melted
2 8-ounce packages cream cheese, softened
1 cup granulated sugar
3 eggs
1 15-ounce can pumpkin
1 egg

¼ cup milk
½ teaspoon ground cinnamon
¼ teaspoon ground ginger
¼ teaspoon ground nutmeg
½ cup whipping cream
    Toasted pecan halves (optional)
    Fresh strawberries (optional)

For crust, stir together graham cracker crumbs, gingersnap crumbs, the 2 tablespoons pecans, flour, powdered sugar, and melted butter in a medium bowl. Press evenly onto the bottom of a 9-inch springform pan; set aside.

Beat cream cheese and granulated sugar in a large mixing bowl with an electric mixer on medium speed until fluffy. Add the 3 eggs all at once; beat on low speed just until combined.

Place 1 cup of the cream cheese mixture in a medium bowl; set

Pea Pods and Onions with Dill Butter

Add a touch of extra color to the meat platter by spooning some vegetables along the side; then place the rest in a separate serving bowl (see photo, page 72).

1 16-ounce package frozen small whole onions*
2 6-ounce packages frozen pea pods
2 cloves garlic, minced, or 1 teaspoon bottled minced garlic
3 tablespoons butter or margarine
1 tablespoon snipped fresh dill or 1 teaspoon dried dillweed
½ teaspoon salt
¼ teaspoon white pepper
    Fresh dill sprigs (optional)

Cook onions in a small amount of boiling water in a large saucepan for

2 minutes. Add pea pods and cook 2 to 3 minutes more or just until tender, stirring occasionally. Drain.**

Meanwhile, cook garlic in hot butter in a small saucepan for 30 seconds. Stir in dill, salt, and white pepper. Drizzle over vegetables, tossing to coat. Garnish with fresh dill sprigs, if desired. Makes 10 to 12 servings.

*****If desired, substitute** 3½ cups fresh pearl onions for the frozen onions. Cook the fresh onions in a small amount of boiling water in a large saucepan for 8 to 10 minutes. Drain and peel onions. Cook pea pods according to package directions. Drain and combine with onions. Continue with recipe at **.

Nutrition facts per serving: 64 cal., 4 g total fat (2 g sat. fat), 9 mg chol., 144 mg sodium, 7 g carbo., 2 g fiber, 2 g pro. **Daily values:** 3% vit. A, 14% vit. C, 2% calcium, 5% iron

Walnut Rolls

Serve these rolls with either the soup or the salad or both (see photo, page 74).

  3 to 3½ cups all-purpose flour
  1 package active dry yeast
  ¾ cup milk
  ¼ cup sugar
  ⅓ cup butter or margarine
  ¼ teaspoon salt
  ¼ teaspoon ground nutmeg
  1 egg
  ⅓ cup finely chopped walnuts
  1 egg white
  1 tablespoon water
  24 walnut halves

Stir 1 cup of the flour and the yeast together in a large bowl; set aside.

Heat milk, sugar, butter, salt, and nutmeg in a small saucepan until warm (120° to 130°) and butter is almost melted. Add to flour mixture. Add egg. Beat with an electric mixer on low speed for 30 seconds, scraping bowl constantly. Beat on high speed for 3 minutes. Stir in chopped walnuts and as much remaining flour as you can with a wooden spoon.

Turn dough out onto a lightly floured surface. Knead in enough of the remaining flour to make a moderately stiff dough that is smooth and elastic (6 to 8 minutes total). Shape into a ball. Place in a lightly greased bowl; turn once to grease surface. Cover and let rise in a warm place until double in size (about 1 hour).

Punch down dough. Turn out onto a lightly floured surface. Divide in half. Cover and let rest 10 minutes. Grease baking sheets. Divide each half of dough into 12 pieces. Roll each piece with your hands into a 12-inch-long rope on a lightly floured surface. Tie each rope into a loose knot, leaving two long ends. Tuck top end under roll. Bring bottom end up and tuck into center of roll. Place 2 to 3 inches apart on prepared baking sheets.

Mix egg white with the water. Brush over tops of rolls. Press a walnut half into center of each roll. Cover and let rise in a warm place until almost double (about 30 minutes).

Bake in a 375° oven for 12 to 15 minutes or until rolls are golden. Transfer rolls to wire racks to cool. Makes 24 rolls.

MAKE-AHEAD TIP: Prepare, bake, and cool rolls. Wrap tightly in foil or place in an airtight container. Freeze the rolls up to 2 months.

Nutrition facts per roll: 123 cal., 6 g total fat (2 g sat. fat), 16 mg chol., 55 mg sodium, 14 g carbo., 1 g fiber, 3 g pro. **Daily values:** 3% vit. A, 0% vit. C, 1% calcium, 5% iron

Prime Rib au Poivre

Anything "au poivre" simply means "with pepper"—and plenty of it. This beautiful roast relies on a rainbow of peppercorn varieties for its piquant crust. Black peppercorns—the most intensely flavored—are simply the dried berries of the pepper plant that are picked when they're not quite ripe; white peppercorns are the dried ripe berries from which the skin has been removed; and pungent, slightly sweet pink peppercorns aren't really pepper berries at all, but the dried berries of a type of rose plant (see photo, page 72).

  1 6- to 8-pound beef rib roast
  2 tablespoons Dijon-style mustard
  2 teaspoons bottled minced garlic
    or 4 cloves garlic, minced
  2 tablespoons whole peppercorns
    (black, pink, and/or white),
    coarsely cracked

Have butcher completely loosen bones for easier carving of roast. Trim any excess fat from top of beef, leaving a layer about ¼ inch thick. Combine mustard and garlic in a small bowl; spread over top of beef. Sprinkle peppercorns over mustard mixture.

Place meat, bone side down and mustard side up, in a foil-lined 15½×10½×2-inch roasting pan. Insert a meat thermometer into center of meat, without touching bone. Roast in a 350° oven until thermometer registers 135° for medium rare (2¼ to 2½ hours) and 150° for medium (2¾ to 3 hours)*. Cover meat with foil. Let meat stand 15 minutes before carving. (The meat's temperature will rise 5 to 10 degrees during standing.) Makes 12 servings.

*****Add squash to oven** when meat is 20° to 25° from desired doneness (115° for medium rare or 130° for medium).

Nutrition facts per serving: 487 cal., 40 g total fat (17 g sat. fat), 114 mg chol., 145 mg sodium, 1 g carbo., 0 g fiber, 29 g pro. **Daily values:** 0% vit. A, 2% vit. C, 1% calcium, 20% iron

79

Hanukkah brings light to the darkest time of the year and joy to the Jews of the world. Challah, cookies, and a fruit-and-nut tart bring sweetness to the celebration.

hanukkah
nights &
delights

The celebration of Hanukkah, the Festival of Lights, commemorates a victory won by the Jews over the Syrian occupiers more than 2,000 years ago. During the eight nights and days of Hanukkah, Jewish people around the world celebrate with special foods. The most commonly eaten foods in America are potato latkes, crisp-fried and served with applesauce. Some people also eat preserve-filled, sugar-coated little doughnuts called *sufganiyot*.

There are other celebratory foods in the Jewish tradition. Challah is a soft, rich bread. Rugelach, a flaky rolled cookie filled with raisins or other dried fruit and nuts, satisfies sweet tooths, as do foods prepared with honey (Israel is "the land of milk and honey"). (Note: According to Jewish law, recipes that include dairy products cannot be eaten alongside or following a meat dish.)

To set a festive table for Hanukkah, cover the table with silver lamé fabric, then lay a runner of blue fabric down the center of the table for color, shaping it slightly for dimension. Arrange a variety of clear glass vases on the runner and fill each with one of the following: hazelnuts in the shell, almonds in the shell, silver-wrapped candies, and blue-foil-wrapped candies. Insert glitter-sprayed dried flowers (from a crafts store or florist's supply shop) into the nuts and candies. Stretch Star-of-David garland (from a party-supply store) along the runner and add candleholders shaped like six-pointed stars.

Challah

82

piece into a 32-inch-long rope. On a greased baking sheet, shape one rope into a triangle; pinch ends together. Form a six-pointed star by weaving the second rope over and under the first triangle, forming a second triangle (as shown below); pinch ends together. Make six 2-inch balls of foil. Place foil in holes that form star points (as shown). Cover; let rise in a warm place until nearly double (about 30 minutes). **Combine egg yolk** and 1 tablespoon water. Brush over loaf. Sprinkle with sesame seed. Bake in a 375° oven about 25 minutes or until bread sounds hollow when tapped, covering with foil after 15 minutes of baking to prevent overbrowning. Remove and cool on a wire rack. Makes 1 loaf (16 servings). **WREATH-SHAPED CHALLAH:** Prepare as above, except divide dough into 3 pieces. Cover and let rest 10 minutes. Shape each piece into a 22-inch-long rope. Loosely braid ropes. Place braided dough onto a greased baking sheet. Form braid into a wreath shape; pinch ends together. Cover and let rise; brush with egg yolk and water, sprinkle with sesame seed, and bake as directed.

Nutrition facts per serving: 133 cal., 4 g total fat (1 g sat. fat), 27 mg chol., 109 mg sodium, 20 g carbo., 1 g fiber, 3 g pro. **Daily values:** 2% vit. A, 0% vit. C, 0% calcium, 7% iron

Challah

✳

This most famous of Jewish yeast breads is most often seen in its traditional braided form. Instead of the braid shape, follow the directions for forming Challah (KHAH-luh) into a star shape.

  1 package active dry yeast
  ¾ cup warm water (110°)
  3 to 3½ cups all-purpose flour
  ¼ cup sugar
  1 egg
  1 egg white
  ¼ cup vegetable oil
  ¾ teaspoon salt
     Pinch ground saffron (optional)
  1 egg yolk
  1 tablespoon water
  2 teaspoons sesame seed

Dissolve yeast in the warm water in a large bowl. Let stand until bubbly (about 5 minutes). Stir in 1¼ cups of the flour, the sugar, egg, egg white, oil, salt, and saffron, if desired. Beat with an electric mixer on low speed for 30 seconds, scraping bowl constantly. Beat on high speed for 3 minutes. Stir in as much remaining flour as you can with a wooden spoon.

Turn dough out onto a lightly floured surface. Knead in enough of the remaining flour to make a moderately soft dough that is smooth and elastic (3 to 5 minutes total). Shape into a ball. Place in a lightly greased bowl; turn once to grease surface. Cover; let rise in a warm place until double (1 hour).

Punch down dough. Divide in half. Cover; let rest 10 minutes. Shape each

here's how...

To help retain the shape of the star as the dough rises and bakes, place 2-inch balls of foil in the holes forming the points of the star, as shown.

Dried Fruit Compote with Sweet Biscuits

A shortcake served with simmered dried fruit makes the perfect ending to a meal.

    1 8-ounce package mixed
          dried fruit
    2½ cups apple juice
    ⅛ teaspoon ground nutmeg
    4 teaspoons cornstarch
    ¼ cup packed brown sugar
    1 teaspoon vanilla
    2 cups all-purpose flour
    2 tablespoons granulated sugar
    1 tablespoon baking powder
    ½ teaspoon salt
    ½ cup vegetable shortening
    1 tablespoon granulated sugar

Snip dried fruit into bite-size pieces. Combine fruit, apple juice, and nutmeg in a medium saucepan. Bring to boiling; reduce heat. Cover and simmer 10 minutes or until fruit is softened. Stir together cornstarch and 2 tablespoons *cold water*. Add to fruit mixture. Cook and stir until thickened and bubbly. Cook and stir 2 minutes more. Stir in brown sugar and vanilla. Remove from heat; set aside.

For biscuits, stir together flour, 2 tablespoons granulated sugar, baking powder, and salt in a large mixing bowl. Cut in shortening until mixture resembles coarse crumbs. Make well in center. Add ⅔ cup *water* all at once. Stir gently with a wooden spoon just until dough clings together.

Knead dough gently 10 to 12 strokes on a lightly floured surface. Roll or pat dough to ½ inch thickness. Cut with a 1½-inch heart-shaped cutter to make 18 biscuits. Transfer to ungreased baking sheet. If desired, using a ½-inch heart-shaped cutter, make indentation in center of each biscuit. Brush biscuits lightly with 1 tablespoon *water* and sprinkle with remaining sugar.

Bake in a 450° oven for 8 to 10 minutes or until lightly browned. Serve warm. Makes 6 servings.

Nutrition facts per serving: 498 cal., 18 g total fat (4 g sat. fat), 0 mg chol., 409 mg sodium, 82 g carbo., 2 g fiber, 5 g pro. **Daily values:** 9% vit. A, 4% vit. C, 16% calcium, 18% iron

Mandel Bread

This crisp bread, sometimes referred to as mandelbrot (mandel meaning "almond" and brot meaning "bread"), is eaten like a cookie. It's similar to Italian biscotti with the double-baking preparation technique.

    ¾ cup sugar
    ¾ cup vegetable oil
    3 eggs
    3 cups all-purpose flour
    1 teaspoon baking powder
    1 cup chopped almonds
    1 cup raisins
    2 teaspoons finely shredded
          lemon peel
    1 teaspoon almond extract

Generously grease a large baking sheet; set aside. Stir together the sugar, oil, and eggs in a large mixing bowl until the sugar dissolves. Combine flour and baking powder. Stir into egg mixture along with nuts, raisins, lemon peel, and almond extract (dough will be sticky). Form dough into two 12×3-inch logs on the prepared baking sheet.

Bake in a 350° oven for 30 minutes. Remove logs from oven and bias-cut into 1-inch-thick slices. Arrange slices on baking sheet. Return to the oven and bake for 10 to 12 minutes more or until lightly browned. Transfer to wire racks to cool. Makes 24 to 28 slices.

Nutrition facts per slice: 196 cal., 11 g total fat (2 g sat. fat), 27 mg chol., 26 mg sodium, 23 g carbo., 1 g fiber, 3 g pro. **Daily values:** 1% vit. A, 1% vit. C, 2% calcium, 5% iron

83

Dried Fruit Compote with Sweet Biscuits

Rugelach

Rugelach

Rugelach (pronounced roo-ge-LAKH) are usually filled with fruits and nuts, poppy seed paste, or preserves. (Note: According to Jewish dietary law, recipes with dairy products may not be eaten along with or following meals featuring meat.)

  1 cup butter or margarine, softened
  2 tablespoons granulated sugar
  1 8-ounce carton dairy sour cream
  1 egg yolk
  2 cups all-purpose flour
  ⅛ teaspoon salt
  ½ cup finely chopped walnuts or pecans
  ½ cup chopped golden raisins
  ½ cup granulated sugar
  ¼ cup butter or margarine, softened
  1½ teaspoons ground cinnamon
    Powdered sugar

For dough, beat the 1 cup butter in a mixing bowl with an electric mixer for 30 seconds. Add the 2 tablespoons sugar; beat until light and fluffy. Add sour cream and egg yolk. Beat well. Stir in flour and salt with a wooden spoon

until combined. Cover and chill 2 hours or until dough is easy to handle.

For filling, combine nuts, raisins, the ½ cup sugar, ¼ cup butter, and the cinnamon; set aside. Divide dough into four portions. Roll one portion of dough to a 10-inch circle. Spread one-fourth of the nut mixture over the circle. Cut dough into 12 wedges. Roll up each wedge, starting at wide end. Repeat. Place 1 inch apart on a foil-lined cookie sheet.

Bake in a 350° oven for 22 to 25 minutes or until edges are lightly browned. Cool on cookie sheet 1 minute. Transfer to wire rack to cool. Sprinkle with powdered sugar. Makes 48 cookies.

Nutrition facts per cookie: 95 cal., 7 g total fat (4 g sat. fat), 19 mg chol., 57 mg sodium, 8 g carbo., 0 g fiber, 1 g pro. **Daily values:** 6% vit. A, 0% vit. C, 0% calcium, 2% iron

Hanukkah Cookies

Cut with a Star of David-shaped cutter, these sugar cookies are made festive with a drizzle or two of blue almond-flavored icing. (See Note under Rugelach.)

  ⅔ cup vegetable shortening
  ¾ cup granulated sugar
  1½ teaspoons baking powder
  ¼ teaspoon salt
  1 egg
  1 tablespoon milk
  ½ teaspoon vanilla
  2 cups all-purpose flour
    Almond Icing

Beat shortening in a large mixing bowl with an electric mixer for 30 seconds. Add sugar, baking powder, and salt; beat until fluffy. Add egg, milk, and vanilla; beat thoroughly. Beat in as much of the flour as you can with the

mixer; stir in any remaining flour with a wooden spoon. Cover and chill dough 1 hour or until it is easy to handle.

Divide dough into three portions. Roll each portion ¼ inch thick on a lightly floured surface. Cut with cookie cutters. Place cookies 1 inch apart on ungreased cookie sheets.

Bake in a 350° oven for 8 to 10 minutes or until edges are lightly browned. Transfer to wire racks to cool. Dip top surface into white Almond Icing. Place on rack set over waxed paper. While icing is moist, drizzle design with blue Almond Icing. Let excess icing drip onto paper. Let cookies stand at room temperature at least 2 hours to allow icing to dry. Makes about 60 (2-inch) cookies.

ALMOND ICING: Stir together 3 cups sifted *powdered sugar*, ⅛ to ¼ teaspoon *almond extract*, and enough *milk* (3 to 4 tablespoons) in a large mixing bowl to make icing of drizzling consistency. Tint one-fourth of the mixture blue with *food coloring.*

Nutrition facts per cookie: 65 cal., 2 g total fat (1 g sat. fat), 4 mg chol., 20 mg sodium, 11 g carbo., 0 g fiber, 1 g pro. **Daily values:** 0% vit. A, 0% vit. C, 0% calcium, 1% iron

Hanukkah Cookies

84

Honey-Pistachio Tart

Honey-Pistachio Tart

Dried fruit-and-nut tarts are a wintertime staple in many culinary traditions. This pistachio-packed tart is rich and dense and infused with the sweet, floral essence of honey. Serve it with full-flavored coffee or hot mint tea.

½ cup sugar
¼ cup honey
¼ cup water
1½ cups chopped pistachio nuts, toasted
½ cup mixed dried fruit bits
¼ cup orange juice
Egg Pastry
1 beaten egg yolk
Coarse sugar

For filling, stir together sugar, honey, and water in a medium saucepan. Bring to boiling, stirring until sugar is dissolved. Reduce heat to medium-low.

Gently simmer, uncovered, 15 minutes or until a light caramel color, stirring occasionally. Stir in pistachios, fruit, and orange juice. Return to boiling; reduce heat. Simmer, uncovered, for 5 minutes or until mixture is slightly thickened, stirring occasionally. Set aside.

Meanwhile, slightly flatten one ball of Egg Pastry into a rectangle. Roll dough into a 16×6-inch rectangle on a lightly floured surface. Wrap around a rolling pin. Unroll onto a 13½×4-inch oblong tart pan with a removable bottom. Ease pastry into pan, pressing it up the fluted sides. Trim pastry even with top edge of pan. Spoon filling evenly into crust.

For top pastry, roll out remaining pastry ball into a 10-inch square. Using a fluted pastry wheel, cut into ½-inch-wide strips. Weave strips diagonally across top of filling for a lattice. Press ends into rim of pan. Brush egg yolk over lattice top and sprinkle with sugar.

Bake in a 375° oven about 35 minutes or until top is golden. (If parts of crust brown more quickly, cover with foil.) Cool in pan on a wire rack. Remove sides from pan. Makes 8 to 12 servings.

EGG PASTRY: Combine 2 cups *all-purpose flour* and ¼ teaspoon *salt* in a large mixing bowl. Cut in ⅔ cup *vegetable shortening* until mixture is the size of small peas. Beat together 1 *egg* and ¼ cup *cold water* in a small bowl. Add egg mixture to flour mixture. Using a fork, toss until dry ingredients are moistened. Divide dough in half. Form each half into a ball.

Nutrition facts per serving: 523 cal., 30 g total fat (6 g sat. fat), 53 mg chol., 84 mg sodium, 57 g carbo., 3 g fiber, 9 g pro. **Daily values:** 7% vit. A, 9% vit. C, 3% calcium, 21% iron

Create a sense of occasion with imaginative table settings.

the art *of the* table

Laying on a holiday table doesn't require special china or linens. Use your collections—blue-and-white china, milk glass, or hotel silver, for example—as your starting point and let color create the mood. Add one element with a holiday motif, such as salad plates, to underscore the seasonal theme.

Autumn Spice

here's how...

Combine rich spice colors to create an autumn-harvest look for Thanksgiving. Start with a tablecloth or layered cloths in warm spice tones. To have extra fabric for catching up at the corners, choose a cloth that's one size larger than your table. Gather up the fabric at each corner and tie it tightly with a long piece of twine. Assemble wheat and cinnamon sticks into four small bouquets and bind them with rubber bands. Tie one bouquet at each corner with the twine, then thread the twine through three dried orange slices and tie in a knot.

Dress the napkins to match by layering each one with an orange slice and tying it in place with twine. For an easy, casual centerpiece, fill three baskets of graduated sizes with fresh and dried fruits and stack them (see page 110). Use dark wicker chargers under the dinner plates to frame the plates and repeat the texture of the baskets.

You can find dried citrus and dried orange slices at crafts stores or florist's supply shops. Or, dry your own slices. Choose firm, good quality fruits. Cut them into slices ¼ inch thick and arrange them on a cooling rack in a 200-degree oven. Let the slices dry for several hours, turning them every hour. After the slices are dry and leathery, turn off the oven, open the oven door slightly, and let the slices cool overnight.

Kwanzaa

 Celebrate history and heritage with a focus on family.

This holiday, observed from December 26 to January 1, celebrates African-American heritage and the strengthening of community through principles of mutual commitment and responsibility. Decorations incorporate symbolic elements, such as the seven-branched candelabrum (called a *kinara*), a straw mat, vegetables, ears of corn, and a communal unity cup.

here's how...

To set a Kwanzaa table, start with the straw mat, which represents tradition as the foundation on which cultural values rest. Vegetables, mounded in shallow baskets, recall the Swahili origins of the word "kwanzaa," which means first fruits of the harvest.

Ears of corn symbolize children and therefore posterity and the future, so they're a perfect base for photo place cards. To make the place cards, start with 18-gauge paper-wrapped florist's wire from a crafts store or florist's supply shop. Thread on decorative beads, then use pliers to bend the wire into geometric shapes at one end, using bends in the wire to space the beads and hold them in place. Trim the straight end of the wire to the desired length. Make a hole in one end of a piece of dried corn (sold as bird or squirrel feed); you may need to use an ice pick for this. Insert the straight end of the place card holder in the hole and secure it with a drop of glue if the wire seems wobbly.

Take pictures with a Polaroid camera of each family member or guest, then insert his or her photo between the bent wires and set the ear of corn at the appropriate place at the table. Or, use the photos as part of the centerpiece, placing them among the fruits and vegetables on the table.

As an added flourish at each place setting, curl a banana leaf or an aspidistra leaf into a cone shape and tie it with raffia. Tuck in a few stems of alstroemeria, a florist's flower that looks like a small lily.

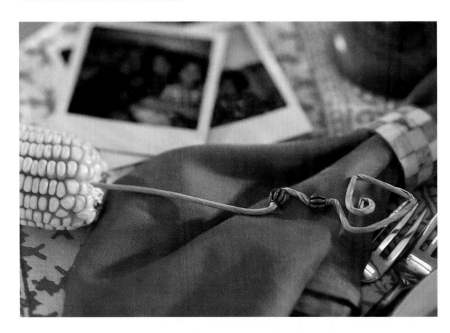

88

Personalized Paper Dolls

here's how...

Family and guests at your Thanksgiving dinner may not be able to resist playing with this centerpiece to create their own three-dimensional vignettes. Go through family photos and select your favorite candid or posed shots. Enlarge them on a color photocopier at least 150 to 200 percent, more if necessary, to obtain figures that are at least 3 to 5 inches tall. Glue the enlargements to card stock with a glue stick, then cut out around the figures. Also include family pets and a picture of your home (or a favorite vacation spot or grandparents' home). Cut pictures of trees and flowers from magazines and glue them to card stock in the same way.

To make the photo holders, buy alligator clips (electric conductors) and 8-gauge bare copper wire from the electrical supply section of a hardware store. (The wire is sold by the foot.) Cut the wire into 4- to 10-inch lengths. Insert one end of each piece of wire into an alligator clip and pinch the clip closed with pliers. Straighten the wire, if you wish, or curl it, using the pliers to grip the wire.

Insert the free end of the wire into winter squash, apples, or oranges (make a starter hole in the winter squash with a hammer and nail).

For more permanent bases, decorate wooden blocks. To make the blocks, buy a 4×4 wooden post at a lumber supply company or home improvement store. Have the store cut the post for you into 4-, 5-, and 6-inch lengths.

Sand the blocks and prime them with white latex paint. Apply two coats of acrylic crafts paint in the colors of your choice—sage green, rust, and tan were used here. After the paint dries, apply a leaf print to one or more sides of each block.

To make the leaf prints, brush metallic copper acrylic crafts paint on the veined side of a fresh leaf. Lay the leaf, paint side down, on the wooden block. Place a sheet of paper on top of the leaf, then rub firmly over the leaf to transfer the paint to the block. Remove the paper, then carefully lift off the leaf, taking care not to smear the paint.

Using a $\frac{1}{8}$-inch drill bit, make a 1- to 2-inch-deep hole in the center of the top of the wooden block. (An easy way to find the center is to draw lines across the block from corner to corner. The point where the diagonals cross is the center.) Insert the wire into the hole.

To create the centerpiece, arrange the blocks and fruits as desired and insert photos. Arrange additional winter squash, miniature pumpkins, and gourds around the photo holders for an autumn table, or use fresh evergreens for a holiday look.

92

Winter Green

here's how...

✎ Bring your love of the garden to the table with pots of evergreens, jute placemats, and dinnerware in soft green tones. Instead of laying the placemats out in the usual way, turn them so the long sides hang over the table's edge; this suggests the effect of a tablecloth and creates a more formal feeling. Soft green dinner plates pick up the green in the holiday salad plates, but you could use plain white dinner plates instead. A simple white napkin with a green organdy edge reinforces the natural color scheme.

To make the place card holders and centerpiece, use aged terra-cotta pots. Or add instant age to new pots by applying a thin coat of green or blue-green acrylic paint and quickly wiping

93

off some of the paint before it dries. You also can let the paint dry and then scuff off paint from the sides and edges with sandpaper. Wedge a piece of water-soaked floral foam into each pot. Stuff in pine tips, holly, or boxwood to make a bouquet. For place settings, use garden markers and write each person's name on the metal marker with an indelible marking pen.

Crocheted toppers for tumblers originally protected iced tea or lemonade from curious insects at outdoor parties or picnics. Bring them indoors for a charming garden touch. To make your own, start with a purchased doily and use thin jeweler's wire to string red and green beads to the points. You can find doilies, wire, and beads at crafts stores.

Bring Out the Silver

Hotel silver is becoming a popular collectible at flea markets and antiques shows, and you can find convincing reproduction pieces at home furnishings shops, too. For a special holiday dinner, bring out all of your silver—baby cups, cream-and-sugar sets, julep cups, trays, and even a foot bath—and use the pieces to set a festive table.

The foot bath, which might have held champagne bottles on ice in a fancy hotel, is ideal for a large arrangement of greenery, lilies, and roses. Arrange smaller bouquets in shaving cups and baby cups, and pile white glass balls in silver ice buckets.

For chargers to frame and present your dinnerware, use a variety of silver trays. Stack plain white china on top,

and wrap the whole with 1-inch-wide red ribbon to make a festive package awaiting guests. For the place card, fold a piece of ivory-color card stock in half and write your guest's name with a calligraphy pen; slip the card over the ribbon and hold it in place with a loop of clear adhesive tape inside the card.

A white lace cloth would make an elegant, formal background for this tabletop, but if you want a richer, more hunt-club feeling, layer green and navy taffeta plaid over the lace. To dress up chairs for the occasion, wrap 2-inch-wide red ribbon around each chair back and tie it in a bow.

Red and White

Mix and match milk glass, patterned china, and hobnail glass to create a cottage-style Christmas tabletop. Spread a red quilt or cloth over the table (make sure the quilt is machine washable in case of spills). Stack red-and-white patterned china and pink hobnail glass plates at each place, and welcome each guest to the table with an individual arrangement of roses in a milk-glass cup, sugar bowl, or creamer. Fill the containers with fresh cranberries to hold the rose stems in place. Add a little water but not enough to make the berries float.

Mix and match flatware too. Check estate sales and antiques shops for inexpensive odd pieces of sterling silver or vintage flatware and combine them for a collected look.

For the centerpiece, create your own epergne by stacking footed candy dishes or vases on a footed cake plate (see page 110 for a closer look). Combine Red Delicious apples, lady apples, red plums and red currants with pink and red roses to emphasize the color theme. For a striking color accent, add purple plums and grapes.

Dress up the backs of chairs with strands of cranberries and tiny red glass balls. Thread fresh or frozen cranberries on dental floss, using a tapestry needle. Since the berries may bleed if they're left out for several hours, tie the garlands to the chairs at the last minute, and then remove them promptly after dinner. Or substitute red wooden beads for the cranberries.

Blue and White

Put your collection of blue-and-white china in a candy-cane-color setting, and you have a merry Christmas breakfast table. Spread a white tablecloth or quilt over the table, then top it with a swath of gingham taffeta. You don't need to cut or sew the taffeta; just buy a length of fabric that's three times the diameter of your table. Fold the fabric in half and lay it across the table, spreading the two halves out on the diagonal (as if you were making a V shape) to cover the tabletop.

Use a large blue-and-white platter to organize a centerpiece of cyclamen and candy-striped candles. For a prettier presentation, slip the cyclamen pots into blue-and-white cachepots or silver plated ice buckets. Add orange fruit, such as persimmons or oranges, around the base of the buckets for a jolt of unexpected color.

Tie napkins with red-and-white gingham ribbon and place a red beaded pear or apple in each coffee cup for a good-morning gift. Place cards certainly aren't necessary, but they can be fun, adding to the sense of occasion. Use rattan balls with pink bows to prop the place card up.

Lunar Liftoff!

Greet the New Year with a glittering futuristic tablescape that suggests rocket ships and moon landings. Spot mirrors from an auto-parts store create the lunar surface.

Layer silver tulle over a white cloth (or if your table is a light color, just use the tulle). Buy blind-spot mirrors in three sizes (2-inch, 3-inch, and 3¾-inch in diameter)—you'll need two or three of each, more if you have a long table. At a discount auto-parts store, the smallest ones cost about $1.50 and the largest about $2.50. Arrange them randomly on the tabletop, along with small votive candles in silver containers.

For a focal point, arrange white flowers in tall, trumpet-shaped vases; if you don't have silver ones, use sleek, clear glass. Choose flowers such as alstroemeria, freesia, or other trumpet-shaped flowers and arrange them in simple, rounded bunches to suggest a spray of fireworks. To reinforce the theme, look for party horns and champagne flutes with elongated shapes and party favors with silver and gold metallic streamers. White napkins and white-and-gold dinner plates complete the lunar look.

Orange-Coconut Triangles
(see recipe, page 103)

Nothing says Christmas so sweetly or succinctly as homemade cookies. Here's a selection to suit every taste, from rich chocolate shortbread to airy nut macaroons to bar cookies you can eat with your hands.

small *and* sweet

cookies 101

Everyone loves a homemade cookie, but tastes and preferences aside, some cookies are decidedly better than others. Here are two pointers to make your cookies the best they can be.

There is some truth to the advertising slogan, "butter is better." Anything on the supermarket shelves labeled "margarine" has to be at least 80 percent vegetable oil or fat—which, if used in baking, will provide decent results. You won't, however, get the distinctive rich flavor and desired texture that butter provides. Certain cookie varieties must contain butter, such as shortbread. Avoid ingredients labeled "spread" that come in a tub, or you'll wind up with sodden or rock-hard cookies. If you do decide to use margarine for cookie baking, particularly for rolled cookie dough, keep in mind that the dough will be softer than if you use butter in your preparations. You may need to chill it in the freezer for a few minutes to make it workable.

For all kinds of baking, it's important that your oven temperature is accurate.

To be sure, set your oven at 350° and let it heat for at least 10 minutes. Put an oven thermometer in place and close the door for at least 5 minutes. If the thermometer registers higher than 350°, reduce the oven setting called for in the recipe by the number of degrees your oven is off. If it's lower, increase the temperature. If your oven is off by more than 50°, have your thermostat adjusted by a qualified repair person.

101

Nut Macaroons
(see recipe, page 103)

keep cookies fresh

Though your holiday cookies may look lovely stored in a pretty cookie jar or decorative tin, there are better ways to help them stay fresh.

■ To store cookies for just a few days, cool them completely. Arrange unfrosted cookies in single layers between sheets of waxed paper. If they're frosted, store them in a single layer or place waxed paper between the layers if the frosting is very firm and dry.

■ Avoid mixing soft and crisp cookies in the same container. The moisture from the soft cookies will make the crisp cookies soggy.

■ Store cookies at room temperature for up to three days. If they're frosted with cream cheese or yogurt icing, refrigerate them.

■ To store cookies long-term, let them cool completely, then package them in freezer bags or airtight containers and freeze for up to three months. Before serving, thaw cookies in the container for 15 minutes. If they are to be frosted, glazed, or sprinkled with sugar, wait until they have thawed completely to decorate them, or your decoration may run or smear.

Snowflakes

Decorate Snowflakes with frosting and a candlewicking pattern. (Candlewicking is a kind of embroidery using French knots and simple stitches.) Fit a decorating tube with a small writing tip. Pipe dots in a pattern, making each dot with a swirl action to look like a knot rather than the usual smooth mound.

102

Snowflakes

These rich, lightly spiced sugar cookies might be named for the form they take, but cut into any other shape, they'll still melt in your mouth.

½ cup butter
⅓ cup shortening
1 cup granulated sugar
⅓ cup dairy sour cream
1 egg
1 teaspoon vanilla
1 teaspoon finely shredded
    lemon peel
¾ teaspoon baking powder
½ teaspoon ground mace
¼ teaspoon baking soda
    Dash salt
2½ cups all-purpose flour
    Powdered Sugar Icing
    Creamy White Frosting

Beat butter and shortening in a large mixing bowl with an electric mixer on medium to high speed for 30 seconds. Add granulated sugar, sour cream, egg,

vanilla, lemon peel, baking powder, mace, baking soda, and salt. Beat until combined. Beat in as much of the flour as you can with the mixer. Stir in any remaining flour with a wooden spoon. Divide dough in half. Cover and chill for 1 to 2 hours or until easy to handle.

Roll each half of dough ⅛ to ¼ inch thick on a well floured pastry cloth. Using 2½- to 3-inch snowflake or star-shape cutters dipped in flour, cut out dough. Use a wide spatula to place cutouts 1 inch apart on an ungreased cookie sheet.

Bake in a 375° oven for 7 to 8 minutes or until edges are firm and bottoms are very lightly browned. Transfer to wire racks to cool. When cool, frost with white or tinted Powdered Sugar Icing. Let dry.

Divide Creamy White Frosting into three or four portions. Leave one white and tint the others the same pale colors used for the icing. Use a small writing tip (1 or 2) on a decorating bag to

decorate iced cookies with a pattern of dots and lines to simulate French knots and stitches (see photo, above). Let stand on wire racks until set. Store cookies in layers separated by waxed paper in a shallow, covered container. Makes about 48 cookies.

POWDERED SUGAR ICING: Combine 2 cups sifted *powdered sugar* and 2 tablespoons *milk* in a small mixing bowl. Stir in additional *milk*, 1 teaspoon at a time, until of drizzling consistency. Tint icing as desired with liquid or paste *food coloring.*

CREAMY WHITE FROSTING: Beat ½ cup *shortening* with an electric mixer on medium speed for 30 seconds. Slowly add 1 cup sifted *powdered sugar,* beating well. Beat in 1 tablespoon *milk.* Gradually beat in 1¼ cups sifted *powdered sugar* and 1 teaspoon *milk.* Add additional milk, 1 teaspoon at a time, until frosting is of spreading consistency. Tint as desired with liquid or paste *food coloring.*

Nutrition facts per cookie: 127 cal., 6 g total fat (2 g sat. fat), 11 mg chol., 39 mg sodium, 18 g carbo., 0 g fiber, 1 g pro. **Daily values:** 2% vit. A, 0% vit. C, 1% calcium, 2% iron

Cardamom-Orange Slices

The edges of these cookie slices are coated with light green pistachio nuts.

½ cup butter, softened
½ cup shortening
1 cup packed brown sugar
1½ teaspoons ground cardamom
1 teaspoon finely shredded
    orange peel
½ teaspoon baking soda
¼ teaspoon salt
1 egg
1 teaspoon vanilla
2½ cups all-purpose flour
¾ cup very finely chopped
    pistachio nuts

Beat butter and shortening in a large mixing bowl with an electric mixer on medium to high speed for 30 seconds. Add brown sugar, cardamom, orange peel, baking soda, and salt. Beat until combined. Add egg and vanilla; beat thoroughly. Beat in as much of the flour as you can with the mixer. Stir in any remaining flour with a wooden spoon.

Shape the dough into two 7-inch-long logs. Roll dough logs in chopped pistachio nuts to coat. Wrap the dough logs in waxed paper or plastic wrap. Chill for 4 to 48 hours.

Cut dough into ¼-inch-thick slices. Place 2 inches apart on an ungreased cookie sheet.

Bake in a 375° oven about 8 minutes or until edges are firm. Cool on cookie sheet for 1 minute. Transfer to wire racks to cool. Makes about 52 cookies.

Nutrition facts per cookie: 81 cal., 5 g total fat (2 g sat. fat), 9 mg chol., 43 mg sodium, 9 g carbo., 0 g fiber, 1 g pro. **Daily values:** 1% vit. A, 0% vit. C, 0% calcium, 3% iron

Nut Macaroons

Hickory nuts are the fruit of trees that grow wild in American woods and forests. The nuts look like tiny pecans and have a similar, rich flavor. If you can't find hickory nuts, pecans make a fine substitute (see photo, page 101).

3 egg whites
¼ teaspoon cream of tartar
1 cup sugar
1 tablespoon all-purpose flour
2 cups finely chopped hickory
    nuts, pecans, or walnuts
    Desired candied fruit pieces,
    such as red or green cherries
    or pineapple wedges

Line two cookie sheets with parchment paper; set aside.

Beat egg whites and cream of tartar in a mixing bowl with an electric mixer until soft peaks form (tips bend over). Gradually add sugar, about 1 tablespoon at a time, beating on high speed until stiff peaks form (tips stand straight). Fold in flour and finely chopped nuts.

Drop mixture by rounded teaspoons 2 inches apart onto the cookie sheets.

Bake in a 400° oven for 5 to 7 minutes or until lightly browned. Cool on cookie sheet for 1 to 2 minutes. Press a piece of candied fruit into the top of each cookie. Transfer to wire racks to cool. Makes about 36 cookies.

Nutrition facts per cookie: 69 cal., 4 g total fat (0 g sat. fat), 0 mg chol., 5 mg sodium, 8 g carbo., 1 g fiber, 1 g pro. **Daily values:** 0% vit. A, 0% vit. C, 0% calcium, 0% iron

Orange-Coconut Triangles

Cut into triangular pieces or bars—it's up to you (see photo, page 100).

½ cup all-purpose flour
¼ cup granulated sugar
¼ cup butter
½ cup finely chopped pecans
2 eggs
¾ cup granulated sugar
2 tablespoons all-purpose flour
1½ teaspoons finely shredded
    orange peel
3 tablespoons orange juice
¼ teaspoon baking powder
1 cup coconut
    Sifted powdered sugar
    (optional)

For crust, combine the ½ cup flour and the ¼ cup sugar in a medium mixing bowl. Cut in butter with a pastry blender until mixture resembles coarse crumbs. Stir in pecans. Press mixture into an ungreased 8×8×2-inch baking pan. Bake in a 350° oven for 18 to 20 minutes or just until golden.

For filling, combine eggs, the ¾ cup sugar, the 2 tablespoons flour, orange peel, orange juice, and baking powder in another medium mixing bowl. Beat 2 minutes with an electric mixer until combined. Stir in coconut.

Pour coconut mixture over baked crust. Bake 20 minutes more or until edges are lightly browned and center is set. Cool in pan on a wire rack.

Cut into 2½-inch squares, then cut each square in half to make triangles or bars. Sprinkle with powdered sugar, if desired. Makes 18 triangles.

Nutrition facts per triangle: 128 cal., 7 g total fat (3 g sat. fat), 31 mg chol., 41 mg sodium, 16 g carbo., 1 g fiber, 2 g pro. **Daily values:** 4% vit. A, 3% vit. C, 1% calcium, 2% iron

103

Double Chocolate-Mint Shortbread

The cool taste of mint is a fitting wintertime treat, and chocolate a celebratory food. Make these melt-in-your-mouth shortbread wedges even more festive with a drizzle of melted chocolate and green candy coating.

¾ cup butter
¾ cup sifted powdered sugar
¼ cup unsweetened cocoa powder
¼ teaspoon mint extract
1⅓ cups all-purpose flour
¾ cup miniature semisweet chocolate pieces
Chocolate-flavored candy coating and/or green vanilla-flavored candy coating, melted (optional)*
Hard candies, crushed (optional)

104

Beat butter in a medium mixing bowl with an electric mixer on medium speed for 30 seconds or until softened. Add powdered sugar, cocoa powder, and mint extract. Beat until smooth. Stir in flour with a wooden spoon until combined. Fold in chocolate pieces. (If necessary, wrap and refrigerate dough a few minutes until easy to handle.)

Lightly grease a cookie sheet. On the prepared cookie sheet, pat the dough into a 9-inch circle. Using your fingers, press to make a scalloped edge. With a fork, prick dough deeply to make 16 wedges.

Bake in a 300° oven about 25 minutes or until edges are firm to the touch and center is set. Let cool for 2 minutes on the cookie sheet. With a long, sharp knife, cut along the fork pricks into wedges. Carefully transfer to a wire rack to cool. Drizzle with melted candy coating and sprinkle with the crushed hard candies before the coating dries, if desired. Makes 16 cookies.

*Tip: If you can't find green candy coating, tint white candy coating with a small amount of green paste food coloring. Dip a toothpick into a little of the paste coloring and stir that amount into the melted coating until the desired shade of green is achieved. (Liquid food coloring may cause the melted candy coating to stiffen.)

Nutrition facts per cookie: 178 cal., 12 g total fat (7 g sat. fat), 25 mg chol., 94 mg sodium, 15 g carbo., 2 g fiber, 1 g pro. **Daily values:** 8% vit. A, 0% vit. C, 1% calcium, 5% iron

Raspberry Cheesecake Bars

What's better than a piece of cheesecake? Why, a piece of cheesecake you can eat with your hands, of course. Try making these bars with apricot preserves for a change of pace.

1¼ cups all-purpose flour
½ cup packed brown sugar
½ cup finely chopped, sliced almonds
½ cup butter-flavored shortening or shortening
2 8-ounce packages cream cheese, softened
⅔ cup granulated sugar
2 eggs
¾ teaspoon almond extract
1 cup seedless raspberry preserves or other preserves or jam
½ cup flaked coconut
½ cup sliced almonds

Combine flour, brown sugar, and the ½ cup finely chopped almonds in a medium mixing bowl. Using a pastry blender, cut in shortening until mixture resembles fine crumbs. Set aside ½ cup crumb mixture for topping.

For crust, press remaining crumb mixture into bottom of an ungreased 13×9×2-inch baking pan. Bake in a 350° oven for 12 to 15 minutes or until the edges are golden brown.

Meanwhile, beat cream cheese, granulated sugar, eggs, and almond extract in another mixing bowl with an electric mixer on low to medium speed until smooth. Spread cream cheese mixture over the hot crust. Return to oven and bake 15 minutes more.

Stir preserves until smooth. Spread over cream cheese mixture. Combine the reserved crumb mixture, the coconut, and sliced almonds in a small mixing bowl. Sprinkle mixture evenly over the preserves.

Double Chocolate-Mint Shortbread

Bake about 15 minutes more or until topping is golden brown. Cool in pan on a wire rack. Cover and chill in the refrigerator for at least 3 hours before cutting into bars. Store, covered, in the refrigerator. Makes 32 bars.

Nutrition facts per bar: 180 cal., 11 g total fat (5 g sat. fat), 29 mg chol., 49 mg sodium, 20 g carbo., 1 g fiber, 3 g pro. **Daily values:** 6% vit. A, 0% vit. C, 2% calcium, 5% iron

Oatmeal-Apricot Drops

½ cup butter
½ cup shortening
1 cup granulated sugar
1 cup packed brown sugar
½ teaspoon baking soda
½ teaspoon salt
2 eggs
2 tablespoons apricot nectar or milk
3 cups all-purpose flour
1¾ cups quick-cooking rolled oats
⅔ cup snipped dried apricots
½ cup chopped pecans
Apricot Glaze

Beat butter and shortening in a large mixing bowl with an electric mixer on medium to high speed for 30 seconds or until softened. Add granulated sugar, brown sugar, baking soda, and salt. Beat until combined. Beat in eggs and apricot nectar until combined. Beat in as much of the flour as you can with a mixer. Stir in any remaining flour, the rolled oats, dried apricots, and pecans with a wooden spoon.

Drop dough by rounded teaspoons about 2 inches apart onto ungreased cookie sheets.

Bake in a 375° oven for 8 to 10 minutes or until edges are lightly browned. Cool on wire racks.

To glaze, place cookies on a wire rack over waxed paper. Drizzle Apricot Glaze over cookies. Let glaze dry. Makes about 66 cookies.

Holiday Toffee Cakes

APRICOT GLAZE: Stir together 2 cups sifted *powdered sugar* and 2 to 3 tablespoons *apricot nectar or milk* in a small mixing bowl to make a glaze of drizzling consistency.

Nutrition facts per cookie: 101 cal., 4 g total fat (1 g sat. fat), 10 mg chol., 43 mg sodium, 16 g carbo., 1 g fiber, 1 g pro. **Daily values:** 2% vit. A, 0% vit. C, 0% calcium, 3% iron

Holiday Toffee Cakes

These confection-studded little cakes are for those sweet tooths who want to have their cookies and their candy too.

2 1.4-ounce packages chocolate-covered toffee pieces (½ cup)
¾ cup butter
⅓ cup sugar
1 tablespoon milk
2 teaspoons vanilla
2¼ cups all-purpose flour
½ cup semisweet chocolate pieces
2 teaspoons shortening

Finely chop chocolate-covered toffee pieces; set aside. Beat butter in a large mixing bowl with an electric mixer on medium to high speed for 30 seconds. Add sugar; beat until combined. Beat in milk and vanilla. Beat in as much flour as you can with the mixer. Stir in remaining flour and the chopped chocolate-covered toffee pieces with a wooden spoon. If necessary, cover and chill 1 hour or until easy to handle.

Shape dough into 1-inch balls. Place the balls of dough 1 inch apart on ungreased cookie sheets.

Bake in a 325° oven for 15 to 20 minutes or until bottoms are lightly browned. Transfer to wire racks to cool.

Combine chocolate pieces and shortening in a small saucepan over low heat. Heat and stir just until chocolate is melted. Drizzle over cookies on plate. Makes about 45 cookies.

Nutrition facts per cookie: 77 cal., 5 g total fat (3 g sat. fat), 10 mg chol., 38 mg sodium, 7 g carbo., 0 g fiber, 1 g pro. **Daily values:** 3% vit. A, 0% vit. C, 0% calcium, 2% iron

Linzertorte
(see recipe, page 108)

new year's in

Vienna has given rise to many great artists, among them the humble bakers and pastry makers who have created some of the world's most famous desserts.

It's said that the Viennese passion for cakes, pastries, and baked goods of all types was set into motion more than 500 years ago, when Emperor Frederick V of Austria ordered that some bread rolls be stamped with his likeness. That simple act apparently started the proverbial ball of dough rolling. Since then, Viennese bakers have created some of the world's most well-known desserts, such as the raspberry-topped Linzertorte and the essence of decadence—rich, chocolate Sachertorte.

What better way, then, to ring in the New Year than with a dessert party featuring a creation of the Viennese, renowned for their appreciation of the finer things in life—the arts, music, and, of course, pastry. Viennese desserts are known not only for their exquisiteness, but also (naturally) for their complexity. Some of these desserts are a bit time-consuming to make, so don't feel embarrassed to make just one.

If you're in the mood for pastry, consider raspberry-filled Linzertorte, which features a Viennese classic—an almond-infused crust. If you lean toward chocolate, make the Almond Sachertorte, an apricot-flavored

PAULA BRONSTEIN / STONE

107

chocoholic's dream. If you have the time and inclination, you might want to offer guests two desserts that provide a nice balance of tastes and textures (for instance, a Sachertorte with a rich, breadlike Gugelhupf).

Champagne is a natural for toasting the New Year, of course, but as Vienna is a city of thousands of coffeehouses (there must be a place to serve all of these sweets, after all), a fitting accompaniment to a Viennese dessert is rich, full-bodied coffee. Consider providing a coffeehouse-style array of complements, including whipped cream, shaved chocolate, and ground cinnamon or nutmeg.

Vienna

Gugelhupf

Tradition calls for this bread, which tastes like cake, to be baked in a Turk's head mold, called so for its turban shape.

⅓ cup golden raisins
⅓ cup raisins or dried cherries
3 tablespoons dark rum, kirsch, or orange juice
2 packages active dry yeast
¼ cup warm water (105° to 115°)
¼ cup butter
½ cup granulated sugar
2 eggs
½ cup warm milk (105° to 115°)
½ teaspoon salt
2½ cups all-purpose flour
1 teaspoon finely shredded lemon peel
1 tablespoon butter, melted
1 tablespoon fine dry bread crumbs
Whole blanched almonds
Sifted powdered sugar (optional)

Combine raisins and rum in a small bowl. Let stand 30 minutes.

Meanwhile, sprinkle yeast over the warm water in a small bowl. Let stand 5 minutes to soften. Beat the ¼ cup butter in a large mixing bowl with an electric mixer on medium to high speed for 30 seconds. Add sugar; beat until combined. Add eggs, one at a time, beating after each. Add yeast mixture, warm milk, and salt, beating until combined. Add 1½ cups of the flour. Beat at medium speed for 2 minutes. Stir in lemon peel, raisin mixture, and remaining flour. Cover; let rise in a warm place until double (about 1 hour).

Brush an 8-inch (6 cup) fluted tube pan generously with the melted butter. Sprinkle evenly with bread crumbs, tapping out any excess crumbs. Arrange almonds in a design in pan; set aside.

Stir down batter. Spoon carefully into prepared pan. Cover and let rise until

almost double (about 45 minutes).

Bake in a 350° oven about 25 minutes or until golden brown. Cool in pan on wire rack for 10 minutes. Unmold onto rack; cool completely. Sprinkle lightly with powdered sugar, if desired. Makes 16 servings.

Nutrition facts per serving: 176 cal., 6 g total fat (3 g sat. fat), 37 mg chol., 129 mg sodium, 26 g carbo., 1 g fiber, 4 g pro. **Daily values:** 5% vit. A, 1% vit. C, 3% calcium, 7% iron

Linzertorte

This raspberry preserve-topped almond tart from the city of Linz is perhaps their most well-known creation (see photo, page 106).

2 hard-cooked egg yolks
⅔ cup butter, softened
⅔ cup sugar
1 egg
1 tablespoon kirsch (cherry brandy) or water
1 teaspoon finely shredded lemon peel
½ teaspoon ground cinnamon
¼ teaspoon ground cloves
1½ cups all-purpose flour
1¼ cups ground almonds or hazelnuts (filberts)
1 12-ounce jar seedless red raspberry jam
1 to 2 tablespoons all-purpose flour
Sifted powdered sugar
Fresh mint sprigs (optional)
Lemon peel curl (optional)

Gently press cooked egg yolks through a fine mesh sieve; set aside.

Beat butter in a medium mixing bowl with an electric mixer on medium to high speed for 30 seconds. Add sugar, egg, hard-cooked yolks, kirsch, lemon peel, cinnamon, and cloves. Beat until thoroughly combined, scraping bowl occasionally. Stir in flour and nuts using a wooden spoon. Form dough into a ball. Wrap in plastic wrap; chill 1 hour.

Use your hands to slightly flatten two-thirds of the dough on a lightly floured surface. (Refrigerate remaining dough until ready to use.) Roll dough from the center to edges, forming an 11-inch circle. Wrap dough around the rolling pin. Then unroll dough onto an ungreased 10×1-inch tart pan with a removable bottom or a 10-inch springform pan. Ease dough into pan, pressing dough about ¾ inch up the sides of the pan. Spread the raspberry jam over the bottom of the dough.

Gently knead an additional 1 to 2 tablespoons flour into remaining dough on a lightly floured surface until dough is easy to handle. Roll dough into a 10×6-inch rectangle. Cut eight strips each about ¾ inch wide, using a fluted pastry wheel, if desired. Lay strips on the filling in an easy lattice pattern (as shown). Trim ends as necessary and gently press ends of strips into rim of bottom crust.

Bake in a 325° oven for 35 to 40 minutes or until crust is golden. Cool in the pan on a wire rack. Remove sides of the tart or springform pan. Before serving, sift powdered sugar over top. Garnish with fresh mint sprigs and

To make easy lattice top on Linzertorte, lay one of the dough strips across the filling, slightly off center (1). Add 3 more strips to form a small square in the center of the torte (2, 3, 4), placing strips about 1 inch apart. Work towards edges with additional strips (5), as shown above.

108

a lightly sugared lemon peel curl, if desired. Makes 10 servings.

Nutrition facts per serving: 432 cal., 23 g total fat (9 g sat. fat), 99 mg chol., 156 mg sodium, 52 g carbo., 3 g fiber, 7 g pro. **Daily values:** 15% vit. A, 2% vit. C, 7% calcium, 10% iron

Almond Sachertorte

This is a close cousin to the famous Viennese torte, traditionally a multilayer chocolate and apricot cake. This version has ground almonds baked inside. Austrian chefs still pipe the word Sacher on this beautiful dessert to indicate that it's the real thing originally created in 1832 by Franz Sacher, whose family owned several famous Viennese hotels and restaurants.

¾ cup butter, softened
⅔ cup sugar
6 egg yolks
6 ounces bittersweet or semisweet chocolate, melted and slightly cooled
¼ cup ground almonds
6 egg whites
¼ teaspoon salt
1 cup all-purpose flour
¾ cup apricot preserves
Chocolate Glaze
¾ cup whipping cream, whipped
Apricot slices (optional)
Chopped almonds (optional)

Grease a 9-inch springform pan and line bottom with waxed paper. Grease paper and lightly coat pan with flour.

Beat butter in a large mixing bowl with an electric mixer on medium speed until smooth and creamy. Gradually add ⅓ cup of the sugar, beating until light and fluffy. Add egg yolks, one at a time, beating after each addition. Beat in melted chocolate and ground almonds.

Wash beaters thoroughly. Beat egg whites and salt until foamy in another large bowl with an electric mixer on medium speed. Gradually beat in

Almond Sachertorte

remaining ⅓ cup sugar. Beat until stiff peaks form (tips stand straight). Fold egg whites into chocolate mixture, one-third at a time, just until combined. Sift in flour, one-third at a time; fold in just until combined. Turn into pan.

Bake in a 350° oven for 35 to 40 minutes or until a wooden toothpick inserted in center comes out clean. Let cake cool 15 minutes. Remove sides of pan and invert cake onto a wire rack set over waxed paper. Remove bottom of pan and peel off waxed paper. Let cake cool completely.

Use a serrated knife to cut cake in half horizontally, making two layers. Remove top layer using two spatulas. Cut up large pieces of apricot preserves. Heat preserves in a small saucepan

until melted; cool slightly. Brush cut side of bottom layer with preserves. Top with second layer, cut side down.

Prepare Chocolate Glaze. Immediately pour glaze over top of cake, spreading, if necessary, to cover top and sides completely. Let stand about 1 hour or until glaze sets. Serve cake with whipped cream. Garnish with apricot slices and chopped almonds, if desired. Makes 12 servings.

CHOCOLATE GLAZE: Combine 3 tablespoons *light-colored corn syrup*, 3 tablespoons *brewed coffee*, and 2 tablespoons *butter* in a medium saucepan. Bring to a boil; remove from heat. Add 6 ounces chopped *bittersweet or semisweet chocolate*. Whisk until melted and smooth.

Nutrition facts per serving: 509 cal., 34 g total fat (19 g sat. fat), 165 mg chol., 246 mg sodium, 52 g carbo., 3 g fiber, 7 g pro. **Daily values:** 25% vit. A, 3% vit. C, 5% calcium, 11% iron

Make your own tiered centerpiece by stacking a milk-glass vase, candy dish, and cake plate. Cluster red and pink roses in the vase and arrange red fruits—pears, apples, grapes, currants, and cranberries—on the remaining tiers. Insert roses into florist's water vials and tuck them among the fruits.

In a Twinkling:
Tables

▲ Prop your place cards on candy-cane easels. Use a hot-glue gun to glue three small canes together along their length, making sure the curved tops rest at the same level.

Fill baskets of graduated sizes with dried fruit, cinnamon sticks, and wheat, then stack them for an easy buffet decoration. For the dining table, arrange them side by side down the center of the table.

◀ Layer cookies and fruit on an old-fashioned tiered dessert stand. You can make your own version of such a stand by stacking footed cake plates and compotes in graduated sizes. Use sticky wax to secure the pieces to each other. Tiered stands let you offer a variety of treats in a small space, and the height of the piece helps create a more interesting table display.

111

◀ Add sparkle and fragrance to the table with a sprig of lavender tucked into a miniature opalescent ornament (remove the hanger to insert the lavender). Tie the ornament to the napkin with organdy ribbon.

Ham and Salsa with
Zucchini Planks
(see recipe, page 114)

112

When the inside oven is full of other holiday foods, fire up the grill for your Christmas feast. Don't let the weather stop you—just follow this wintertime grilling advice, then select one of the festive main dishes that fits the season.

winter grilling

grilling 101

Grilling is a great way to cook—it keeps the kitchen less chaotic, and it infuses food with a wonderful, smoky flavor. Although it's easy, there's more to it than simply tossing some shrimp on the "barbie" and watching it cook.

There are two methods of grilling, whether you're using a gas or a charcoal grill. One is called direct grilling. This means the food is placed on the rack directly over the heat. Direct grilling is used for fast-cooking foods such as burgers, boneless chicken, and fish.

Indirect grilling means a covered grill acts as an oven. A disposable drip pan is placed in the center of the charcoal grate and the hot coals are arranged around it. This method is used for slower-cooking foods, such as roasts and bone-in poultry.

For indirect grilling on a gas grill, light the grill according to the manufacturer's directions. Turn the setting to high and let the grill preheat, covered, for 10 to 15 minutes. Reduce the heat on one burner to medium or medium-high, depending on the recipe, and turn the other burner off to set up two heat zones. Place the drip pan directly on the lava rocks, ceramic briquettes, or

flavorizer bars on the burner that's turned off. If your gas grill has a built-in drip pan or grease catcher, you won't need to add one. Otherwise, use a disposable foil pan or make your own with heavy-duty foil. Adjust the gas flow to the burner that's on to maintain the desired temperature. Place food on the grill rack directly over the drip pan. (If food is placed in a roasting pan, a drip pan isn't needed.)

For longer-cooking foods on a charcoal grill, you may need to add

charcoal every 20 to 30 minutes to maintain the heat. Here's a low-tech way to tell the approximate temperature of your coals: Hold your hand over the area where the food will cook for as long as you comfortably can and count while you hold. The number of seconds you can keep your hand over the heat will give you a clue. A 2-second hand count means the coal temperature is *high*, 3 seconds is *medium-high*, 4 seconds is *medium,* and 6 seconds means the coal temperature is *low*.

wintertime grilling

For those who live in the Southernmost states, wintertime grilling is really no different from summertime grilling. But if you live in a cold-weather climate, consider these suggestions when grilling outdoors in the winter:

■ Don't grill on a windy day. If you're using a charcoal grill, your coals may not stay lit, and on a gas grill, the flame might blow out.

■ Use the indirect grilling method if you can. It employs a covered grill and is a more hands-off method of grilling so you're not running in and out of the cold to check on dinner.

■ Allow slightly longer cooking times than specified in the recipe. The timings for most grill recipes are based on grilling outdoors on a still, 70° day. A low outdoor temperature may mean your foods need a little longer to cook. Use a meat thermometer to check the doneness of the food. You don't want to undercook the food, but you don't want to leave it out there to get dry and overdone, either.

Ham and Salsa with Zucchini Planks

Check the ham label. If the ham is only partially cooked, increase grilling time as necessary until a meat thermometer inserted into the center of the ham slice reaches 160° (see photo, page 112).

  1 pink or red grapefruit, peeled, sectioned, seeded, and cut up
  1 orange, peeled, sectioned, seeded, and cut up
  ⅓ cup canned crushed pineapple, drained
  2 tablespoons sliced green onion
  2 tablespoons chopped red sweet pepper
  1 small fresh jalapeño or habañero pepper, seeded and finely chopped*
  1 tablespoon honey
  1 1½- to 2-pound fully cooked center-cut ham slice, cut about 1 inch thick
  1 pound medium zucchini, ends trimmed and sliced on the bias about ¼ to ½ inch thick
  1 tablespoon olive oil or cooking oil
  2 teaspoons sesame seed, toasted (optional)

For salsa, combine grapefruit, orange, pineapple, green onion, sweet pepper, chili pepper, and honey in a small mixing bowl. Cover and chill the mixture up to 2 hours.

Trim fat from ham. Slash edges of ham at 1-inch intervals. Brush zucchini with the oil; set aside. For a charcoal grill, grill ham slice on the rack of an uncovered grill directly over medium-hot coals for 8 minutes. Turn ham slice over and add zucchini to grill rack. Continue grilling about 10 minutes more or until ham is heated through

and zucchini is tender, turning zucchini over once. [For a gas grill, preheat grill. Reduce heat to medium-hot. Place ham and zucchini on grill rack over the heat, cover, and grill as directed at left.]

To serve, cut the ham into serving-size pieces. Spoon the salsa over the ham and serve with the zucchini. Sprinkle with toasted sesame seed, if desired. Makes 6 servings.

*NOTE: Because chili peppers contain very pungent oils, protect your hands when preparing fresh chili peppers. Put gloves or sandwich bags over your hands so your skin doesn't come in contact with the peppers. Don't touch your eyes, and always wash your hands and nails thoroughly in hot, soapy water after handling chili peppers.

Nutrition facts per serving: 221 cal., 8 g total fat (2 g sat. fat), 53 mg chol., 1,624 mg sodium, 14 g carbo., 2 g fiber, 23 g pro. **Daily values:** 6% vit. A, 88% vit. C, 4% calcium, 8% iron

---

Blue-Cheese-Stuffed Pork Chops

  ½ cup shredded carrot
  ¼ cup chopped pecans
  ¼ cup crumbled blue cheese
  1 green onion, thinly sliced
  1 teaspoon Worcestershire sauce
  4 pork loin or rib chops, cut 1¼ inches thick (about 2¼ pounds total)
  ¼ cup plain yogurt
  4 teaspoons all-purpose flour
  ¾ cup milk
  ½ teaspoon instant chicken bouillon granules
     Dash pepper
     Chopped pecans (optional)
     Crumbled blue cheese (optional)

Combine carrot, the ¼ cup pecans, the ¼ cup blue cheese, the onion, and Worcestershire sauce in a small mixing bowl; set aside.

Trim fat from chops. Make a pocket in each chop by cutting horizontally into the chop from the fat side almost to the bone. Spoon about ¼ cup of the stuffing into each pocket. If necessary, securely fasten the opening with wooden toothpicks.

For a charcoal grill, arrange medium-hot coals around a drip pan for indirect cooking in a covered grill. Test for medium heat above the pan. Place chops on the grill rack over the drip pan. Cover and grill for 35 to 40 minutes or until juices run clear, turning once. [For a gas grill, preheat grill. Reduce heat to medium. Adjust for indirect cooking (see page 113) and grill as above.]

For sauce, stir together yogurt and flour in a small saucepan. Add milk, bouillon granules, and pepper. Cook and stir until thickened and bubbly. Cook and stir for 1 minute more.

To serve, remove toothpicks from chops and serve sauce over chops. Sprinkle with additional chopped pecans and crumbled blue cheese, if desired. Makes 4 servings.

Nutrition facts per serving: 326 cal., 19 g total fat (6 g sat. fat), 87 mg chol., 334 mg sodium, 8 g carbo., 1 g fiber, 29 g pro. **Daily values:** 44% vit. A, 8% vit. C, 11% calcium, 9% iron

---

Chutney Roast

You'll need nothing but a butter knife to cut into this meltingly tender beef tenderloin. Perfect for a special occasion, this king of roast beef is crowned with an exotic chutney crust.

  ⅓ cup unsweetened pineapple juice
  ¼ cup steak sauce or Worcestershire sauce
  3 tablespoons orange juice
  2 tablespoons lemon juice

114

1½ teaspoons sugar
½ teaspoon lemon-pepper
   seasoning
1   2½- to 3-pound beef tenderloin
½ cup chutney

For marinade, combine pineapple juice, steak sauce or Worcestershire sauce, orange juice, lemon juice, sugar, and lemon-pepper seasoning in a small mixing bowl. Place meat in a plastic bag set in a shallow dish. Pour marinade over meat in bag. Seal bag and turn meat to coat well. Marinate in the refrigerator for 6 to 12 hours, turning bag occasionally.

Remove meat from bag, reserving marinade. Chill marinade while grilling meat. Insert meat thermometer near the center of the roast.

For a charcoal grill, arrange medium-hot coals for indirect cooking in a covered grill. Test for medium heat where meat will cook. Place meat on a rack in a roasting pan on the grill rack. Cover and grill for 30 minutes or until meat thermometer registers 135°, brushing with reserved marinade halfway through grilling time. Discard any remaining marinade.

Cut up any large pieces of chutney; spoon chutney evenly over the meat. Cover and grill to desired doneness. Allow 35 to 45 minutes total time for 140° (rare) and 45 to 60 minutes total time for 145° (medium-rare). [For a gas grill, preheat grill. Reduce heat to medium. Adjust for indirect cooking (see page 113) and grill on rack in pan as above.] Slice the beef tenderloin to serve. Makes 10 servings.

Nutrition facts per serving: 203 cal., 7 g total fat (3 g sat. fat), 64 mg chol., 212 mg sodium, 11 g carbo., 0 g fiber, 22 g pro. **Daily values:** 0% vit. A, 8% vit. C, 0% calcium, 18% iron

Double-Glazed
Turkey Breasts

Double-Glazed Turkey Breasts

Instead of roasting a turkey in the oven for the holiday meal, try grilling turkey breasts. Go one step further and give your guests a choice of glaze.

⅔ cup orange marmalade
2 tablespoons hoisin sauce
½ teaspoon five-spice powder
½ teaspoon garlic powder
½ cup honey
2 tablespoons Dijon-style mustard
2 tablespoons white wine
   Worcestershire sauce
2 tablespoons butter or
   margarine, melted
2   2- to 2½-pound turkey breast
   halves
1 tablespoon cooking oil
   Orange peel curls

For five-spice glaze, stir together marmalade, hoisin sauce, five-spice powder, and garlic powder in a small mixing bowl; set aside.

For honey-mustard glaze, stir together honey, mustard, Worcestershire sauce, and butter in a

small mixing bowl; set aside. Reserve half of each glaze in separate bowls

Remove bones from turkey breasts. Brush turkey with oil. Insert a meat thermometer into the center of one of the turkey breasts.

For a charcoal grill, arrange medium-hot coals around a drip pan for indirect cooking in a covered grill. Test for medium heat above pan. Place turkey breasts, side by side, on grill rack over drip pan. Cover; grill for 1½ to 2 hours or until thermometer registers 170°, brushing one breast half with five-spice glaze and the other with honey-mustard glaze several times the last 15 minutes of grilling. If necessary, add extra coals every 20 to 30 minutes to maintain heat. Brush turkey again before serving, if desired. [For a gas grill, preheat grill. Reduce heat to medium. Adjust for indirect cooking (see page 113) and grill as above.] Heat reserved glazes; pass with sliced turkey. Garnish with orange peel curls, if desired. Makes 8 servings.

Nutrition facts per serving: 458 cal., 15 g total fat (5 g sat. fat), 113 mg chol., 327 mg sodium, 38 g carbo., 1 g fiber, 41 g pro. **Daily values:** 2% vit. A, 2% vit. C, 3% calcium, 15% iron

▶ Potato Cutouts: Thinly slice a white potato. Cut several potato slices into shapes using small holiday cookie or hors d'oeuvre cutters. In a small skillet or saucepan cook slices in a small amount of oil until golden brown and crisp. Use the potato cutouts as a garnish for vegetable side dishes or cream soups.

▼ Herb-Topped Rolls: To decorate brown-and-serve dinner rolls, brush the unbaked rolls with a mixture of 1 egg white beaten with a tablespoon of water. While the mixture is still moist, place a small sprig of fresh Italian parsley or other small herb leaves on the rolls. Brush again with the egg-white mixture before baking.

◀ Orange Cups: Remove a very thin slice from the top and bottom of a large navel orange so it will sit flat; slice the orange in half. Use a paring or grapefruit knife and melon baller to remove the flesh from the orange. Orange cups can be used to serve cranberry sauce or chutney. Or, freeze cups and fill with sorbet or other frozen desserts.

In a Twinkling:
Garnishes

116

◀ Festive Appetizer: Spoon guacamole and salsa into several margarita glasses, serving one glassful at a time and keeping the rest refrigerated for replenishing the appetizer table. To prepare, rub the rims of glasses with a lime slice, then dip them into coarse salt. Spoon in guacamole. Fill small bowls (such as votive candleholders) with salsa and press them into the guacamole. (Insert them off-center to allow more room for dipping.) Set on a flat, napkin-lined basket and surround with tortilla chips. Garnish the rim of the glass with a thin lime slice.

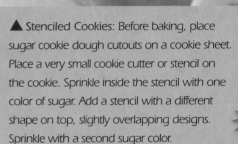

◄ Punch Bowl Garnish: To chill punch, freeze a shallow layer of fruit juice in a ring mold. Arrange fruit, such as very thin lime half-slices and fresh cranberries, atop the frozen layer in the mold. Add about 1 inch of fruit juice to hold the fruit in place as it freezes. When frozen, add additional fruit juice to fill the mold and freeze it solid. Unmold and float it in punch.

▲ Stenciled Cookies: Before baking, place sugar cookie dough cutouts on a cookie sheet. Place a very small cookie cutter or stencil on the cookie. Sprinkle inside the stencil with one color of sugar. Add a stencil with a different shape on top, slightly overlapping designs. Sprinkle with a second sugar color.

► Cheese Ball: Spruce up your favorite cheese ball by rolling half of it in a mixture of snipped dried cranberries or cherries. Roll the other half in chopped pistachio nuts. Make sure you roll the ball along a straight edge so there's a definite division where the two ingredients meet.

◄ Quick Champagne Cocktail: Add a dash of fruit liqueur to a champagne flute, then carefully pour in champagne. Garnish with a long strip of orange peel (made with a zester) that's been curled tightly around a bamboo skewer. For an alcohol-free version, substitute carbonated water for the champagne and fruit-flavored syrup for the liqueur.

Almond Brunch Loaf

118

With a bread machine, you can start on a coffee cake or dinner rolls while you're trimming the tree or wrapping presents.

bread-machine *bounty*

Almond Brunch Loaf

Lovely to look at and even better to eat, this orange-almond coffee cake will be the hit of the party. Serve it with fresh-squeezed orange juice and rich, full-bodied coffee.

1½ pound 12 servings	INGREDIENTS	2 pound 16 servings
½ cup	milk	⅔ cup
1 teaspoon	finely shredded orange peel	1¼ teaspoons
¼ cup	orange juice	⅓ cup
1	egg	1
2 tablespoons	butter or margarine, cut up	3 tablespoons
3 cups	bread flour	4 cups
1 tablespoon	sugar	4 teaspoons
¾ teaspoon	salt	1 teaspoon
1½ teaspoons	bread machine yeast or active dry yeast	1¾ teaspoons
⅔ cup	almond cake and pastry filling (not almond paste)	1 cup
3 tablespoons	chopped toasted almonds	⅓ cup
½ teaspoon	finely shredded orange peel	½ teaspoon
1 tablespoon	orange juice	1 tablespoon
2 teaspoons	sugar	2 teaspoons

Select recipe size. Add milk, first measure of orange peel and orange juice, egg, butter, flour, first measure of sugar, salt, and yeast to a bread machine according to the manufacturer's directions. Select the dough cycle. When the dough cycle is complete, remove dough from machine. Punch down. Cover and let rest for 10 minutes.

For filling, combine almond filling, almonds, and remaining ½ teaspoon orange peel; set aside. Lightly grease a baking sheet. Roll the 1½-pound recipe into a 24×8-inch rectangle on a lightly floured surface. (For the 2-pound recipe, roll dough into a 24×12-inch rectangle.) Spread filling over the dough to within ½ inch of the edges.

Fold dough loosely, starting from a short side, making 3-inch-wide folds (see photo 1). Transfer to prepared baking sheet. On one of the long sides, make eleven cuts for the 1½-pound recipe (15 cuts for the 2-pound recipe) from edge almost to, but not through, the other side, at about ¾-inch intervals.

Flip every other strip of dough over to the opposite side, slightly twisting each strip and exposing the filling (see photo 2); pull slightly to flatten. Cover and let rise in a warm place until nearly double (about 30 minutes).

Bake in a 350° oven about 30 minutes or until bread sounds hollow when lightly tapped. Cover loosely with foil after 20 minutes of baking to prevent overbrowning. Brush baked bread with the 1 tablespoon orange juice and sprinkle with the 2 teaspoons sugar. Cool on a wire rack.

Nutrition facts per serving (¹/₁₂): 229 cal., 6 g total fat (2 g sat. fat), 24 mg chol., 184 mg sodium, 39 g carbo., 3 g fiber, 6 g pro. **Daily values:** 3% vit. A, 6% vit. C, 2% calcium, 12% iron

here's how...

119

Make a series of folds in the dough that are 3 inches wide, starting from one of the short sides.

After making cuts along one side almost to the other, pull and flip every other strip of dough to the opposite side. Slightly pull and twist each so the cut side is facing up.

Cheddar Cheese Bows

each half of dough into a16×12-inch rectangle; cut into sixteen 12×1-inch strips.)

Grease or line baking sheets with foil. Shape each strip into a bow on baking sheet following directions in photo, below. Press dough together at center. Cover; let rise in a warm place until nearly double (20 to 30 minutes). Brush with additional milk and sprinkle lightly with poppy seed. Bake in 375° oven 12 minutes or until golden. Cool on racks.

LOAF: Select basic white bread cycle. If available, select light-crust color setting. Omit brushing with milk and sprinkling with seed. (For 1½-pound loaf, the bread machine pan must have a capacity of 10 cups or more. For the 2-pound loaf, the bread machine pan must have a capacity of 12 cups or more.)

*NOTE: Our Test Kitchen recommends 1 egg for either size.

Nutrition facts per roll (¹/₂₄): 100 cal., 3 g total fat (1 g sat. fat), 16 mg chol., 112 mg sodium, 14 g carbo., 0 g fiber, 4 g pro. **Daily values:** 2% vit. A, 0% vit. C, 4% calcium, 5% iron

Cheddar Cheese Bows

Made into a loaf, this mouthwatering cheese bread can be sliced and paired with leftover Christmas ham or roast beef for terrific sandwiches when the cook needs a night off.

here's how...

To shape bows, work on the baking sheet. Form two loops; bring ends to the center and overlap the tails about 1½ inches. Twist the tails together once and press at center against the baking sheet.

1½ pound 24 rolls	INGREDIENTS	2 pound 32 rolls
1 cup	milk	1¼ cups
1	egg*	1
3 cups	bread flour	4 cups
1¼ cups	shredded cheddar, Swiss, or Monterey Jack cheese	1⅔ cups
2 tablespoons	sugar	3 tablespoons
¾ teaspoon	salt	1 teaspoon
1 teaspoon	bread machine yeast or active dry yeast	1¼ teaspoons
	Milk	
	Poppy seed	

Select recipe size. Add milk, egg, flour, cheese, sugar, salt, and yeast to a bread machine according to directions.

ROLLS: Select the dough cycle. When cycle is complete, remove dough from machine. Punch down. Cover; let rest for 10 minutes. Divide dough in half. Roll each half of 1½-pound recipe into a 12-inch square on a lightly floured surface. Cut into twelve 12×1-inch strips. (For the 2-pound recipe, roll

bread machine basics

Although using a bread machine may be a nearly fool-proof way to turn out delicious, fresh bread from your very own kitchen, there are a few things you can do to help assure that your breads are the best they can be.

■ Use bread flour rather than all-purpose flour. Bread flour has more gluten, a type of protein in flour that gives bread dough its elastic consistency. Gluten traps bubbles of carbon dioxide that form when the yeast eats the sugars in the dough. The more gluten in the dough, the higher bread will rise, and the better structural form it will have.

■ If you store flour or grains in the freezer, warm the measured amount to room temperature before using.

■ Store opened yeast in the refrigerator after opening— and be sure to use it before the expiration date stamped on the package or jar.

Ginger Pumpkin Bread

1½ pound** 16 slices	INGREDIENTS	2 pound** 22 slices
½ cup	milk	⅔ cup
½ cup	canned pumpkin	⅔ cup
1	egg*	1
2 tablespoons	butter or margarine, cut up	3 tablespoons
3 cups	bread flour	4 cups
1 tablespoon	brown sugar	2 tablespoons
¾ teaspoon	salt	1 teaspoon
¼ teaspoon	ground nutmeg	½ teaspoon
1 teaspoon	active dry yeast or bread machine yeast	1¼ teaspoons
½ cup	snipped pitted dates	⅔ cup
2 tablespoons	finely chopped crystallized ginger	3 tablespoons

Select recipe size. Add ingredients to a bread machine according to directions. Select the basic white bread cycle.
***Note:** Our Test Kitchen recommends 1 egg for either size.
****Note:** For 1½-pound loaf, the bread machine pan must have a capacity of 10 cups or more. For the 2-pound loaf, the bread machine pan must have a capacity of 12 cups or more.

Nutrition facts per slice (¹/₁₆): 139 cal., 2 g total fat (1 g sat. fat), 18 mg chol., 126 mg sodium, 25 g carbo., 1 g fiber, 4 g pro. **Daily values:** 19% vit. A, 1% vit. C, 1% calcium, 9% iron

Wheat Cloverleaf Rolls

1½ pound 16 rolls	INGREDIENTS	2 pound 24 rolls
¾ cup	buttermilk	1 cup
1	egg(s)	2
¼ cup	butter or margarine, cut up	⅓ cup
1½ cups	bread flour	2 cups
1½ cups	whole wheat flour	2 cups
2 tablespoons	sugar	3 tablespoons
¾ teaspoon	salt	1 teaspoon
1 teaspoon	bread machine yeast or active dry yeast	1¼ teaspoons
1	egg white	1
1 tablespoon	water	1 tablespoon
	Sesame seed	

Select recipe size. Add buttermilk, egg(s), butter, flours, sugar, salt, and yeast to bread machine according to directions.

Rolls: Select the dough cycle. When cycle is complete, remove dough from machine. Punch down. Cover and let rest for 10 minutes. Lightly grease 16 muffin cups (grease 24 cups for 2-pound recipe). Divide dough in half. For the 1½-pound recipe, divide each half into 24 pieces for a total of 48 pieces. (For 2-pound recipe, shape each half into 36 pieces for a total of 72 pieces.) Shape each piece into a ball. **Place 3 balls in each muffin cup.** Stir together egg white and water in a small mixing bowl; brush over rolls. Sprinkle rolls lightly with sesame seed. Cover and let rise in a warm place until nearly double (20 to 25 minutes).
Bake in a 375° oven for 12 to 15 minutes or until golden brown. Serve warm.
Loaf: Select the whole grain or basic white bread cycle. Omit brushing with water and sprinkling with sesame seed. (For 1½-pound loaf, the bread machine pan must have a capacity of 10 cups or more. For the 2-pound loaf, the bread machine pan must have a capacity of 12 cups or more.)

Nutrition facts per roll (¹/₁₆): 129 cal., 4 g total fat (2 g sat. fat), 21 mg chol., 149 mg sodium, 20 g carbo., 2 g fiber, 4 g pro. **Daily values:** 3% vit. A, 0% vit. C, 1% calcium, 6% iron

Banana-Chocolate Chip Bread

1½ pound** 16 slices	INGREDIENTS	2 pound** 22 slices
½ cup	milk*	½ cup
½ cup	mashed ripe banana	⅔ cup
1	egg(s)	2
2 tablespoons	butter or margarine, cut up*	2 tablespoons
3 cups	bread flour	4 cups
2 tablespoons	brown sugar	3 tablespoons
¾ teaspoon	salt	1 teaspoon
1 teaspoon	active dry yeast or bread machine yeast	1¼ teaspoons
⅓ cup	miniature semisweet chocolate pieces	½ cup

Select recipe size. Add the ingredients to a bread machine according to manufacturer's directions. Select the basic white bread cycle.
***Note:** Our Test Kitchen recommends ½ cup milk and 2 tablespoons butter or margarine for either size loaf.
****Note:** For 1½-pound loaf, the bread machine pan must have a capacity of 10 cups or more. For the 2-pound loaf, the bread machine pan must have a capacity of 12 cups or more.

Nutrition facts per slice (¹/₁₆): 145 cal., 3 g total fat (1 g sat. fat), 18 mg chol., 126 mg sodium, 25 g carbo., 1 g fiber, 4 g pro. **Daily values:** 2% vit. A, 1% vit. C, 1% calcium, 8% iron

Easy Christmas Stollen

The traditional shape for this German holiday bread is similar to the coin-purse shape of Parker House rolls. Decorate the top with additional candied fruit, if you like.

1½ pound 12 servings	INGREDIENTS	2 pound 16 servings
1 cup	milk	1¼ cups
2 teaspoons	finely shredded lemon peel	1 tablespoon
1	egg*	1
2 tablespoons	butter or margarine, cut up	3 tablespoons
3 cups	bread flour	4 cups
2 tablespoons	sugar	3 tablespoons
¾ teaspoon	salt	1 teaspoon
½ teaspoon	ground nutmeg	¾ teaspoon
1½ teaspoons	bread machine yeast or active dry yeast	2 teaspoons
½ cup	chopped candied red and/or green cherries and/or candied pineapple	¾ cup
¼ cup	dark raisins	⅓ cup
¼ cup	chopped toasted almonds	⅓ cup
	Powdered Sugar Icing	
	Candied fruit (optional)	

Select recipe size. Add milk, lemon peel, egg, butter, flour, sugar, salt, nutmeg, and yeast to a bread machine according to the manufacturer's directions. Select the dough cycle. When the dough cycle is complete, remove dough from machine. Punch down. Cover and let rest for 10 minutes.

Roll dough to a 12-inch square on a lightly floured surface. Sprinkle candied fruit, raisins, and nuts over dough. Fold over one side to center. Fold opposite side over folded side to form 3 layers. Cut dough in half crosswise.

Grease a baking sheet. Roll each portion of the 1½-pound dough into an 8×5½-inch rectangle. (For the 2-pound recipe, roll each portion of the dough into a 9×6-inch rectangle.) Brush top of dough lightly with water. Without stretching, fold a long side over to within 1 inch of opposite side; press edges lightly to seal. Place on baking sheet. Cover and let rise in a warm place until nearly double (45 to 60 minutes).

Bake in a 375° oven for 20 to 25 minutes or until golden and loaf sounds hollow when tapped. Cover loosely with foil the last 10 minutes of baking, if necessary, to prevent overbrowning. Remove from baking sheet and cool on a wire rack. Frost with Powdered Sugar Icing and decorate with candied fruit, if desired. Each recipe makes 2 loaves.

POWDERED SUGAR ICING: Stir together ¾ cup sifted *powdered sugar*, ½ teaspoon *vanilla*, and enough *milk* (about 2 teaspoons) in a small mixing bowl to make an icing of spreading consistency.

*****NOTE:** Our Test Kitchen recommends 1 egg for either size.

Nutrition facts per serving (¹⁄₁₂): 236 cal., 5 g total fat (2 g sat. fat), 25 mg chol., 188 mg sodium, 42 g carbo., 1 g fiber, 6 g pro. **Daily values:** 4% vit. A, 1% vit. C, 4% calcium, 11% iron

Sweet Cardamom Braid

Scandinavian bakers love the warm, spicy-sweet taste of cardamom in all sorts of breads and cookies at this time of year.

1½ pound 12 servings	INGREDIENTS	2 pound 16 servings
½ cup	milk	¾ cup + 1 tablespoon
¼ cup	dairy sour cream	⅓ cup
1	egg*	1
3 tablespoons	butter or margarine, cut up	¼ cup
3 cups	bread flour	4 cups
¼ cup	granulated sugar	⅓ cup
1¼ teaspoons	ground cardamom	1½ teaspoons
¾ teaspoon	salt	1 teaspoon
1½ teaspoons	bread machine yeast or active dry yeast	2 teaspoons
1	egg*	1
1 tablespoon	water	1 tablespoon
	Granulated sugar	
	Powdered Sugar Icing	
2 tablespoons	toasted sliced almonds	2 tablespoons

Select recipe size. Add milk, sour cream, 1 egg, butter, flour, the first sugar, cardamom, salt, and yeast to a bread machine according to the manufacturer's directions. Select the dough cycle. When the dough cycle is complete, remove dough from machine. Punch down. Cover and let rest for 10 minutes. For the 1½-pound recipe, divide dough into thirds; shape each piece into an 18-inch rope. (For the 2-pound recipe, divide dough into 6 equal pieces; shape each piece into a 14-inch rope.)

Grease large baking sheet(s). Place 3 ropes, 1 inch apart on prepared baking sheet. Braid ropes loosely, starting at the center and braiding towards each end. Pinch ends together and tuck under. (For the 2-pound recipe, repeat braiding with remaining 3 ropes, making 2 braids total.) Cover and let rise in a warm place until nearly double (about 45 minutes).

Beat remaining egg and water in a small cup. Brush braid(s) with egg mixture; sprinkle generously with sugar.

122

Bake in a 375° oven about 25 minutes for large loaf and 20 to 25 minutes for smaller loaves or until bread sounds hollow when tapped. Cover loosely with foil the last 5 minutes of baking, if necessary, to prevent overbrowning. Remove from baking sheet and cool on a wire rack. Drizzle with Powdered Sugar Icing and sprinkle with almonds.

POWDERED SUGAR ICING: Stir together ¾ cup sifted *powdered sugar* and ½ teaspoon *vanilla* in a small bowl. Add enough *milk* (2 to 3 teaspoons) to make drizzling consistency.

*NOTE: Our Test Kitchen recommends 1 egg for either size.

Nutrition facts per serving (¹⁄₁₂): 230 cal., 6 g total fat (3 g sat. fat), 46 mg chol., 196 mg sodium, 37 g carbo., 1 g fiber, 6 g pro. **Daily values:** 6% vit. A, 0% vit. C, 3% calcium, 10% iron

Holiday Eggnog Bread

Holiday Eggnog Bread

Here are all the tastes of Christmas—eggnog, nutmeg, and candied fruits and peels—in one beautiful loaf.

1½ pound** 12 slices	INGREDIENTS	2 pound** 16 slices
½ cup	canned or dairy eggnog	¾ cup
¼ cup	water	⅓ cup
1	egg*	1
2 tablespoons	butter or margarine, cut up	3 tablespoons
3 cups	bread flour	4 cups
2 tablespoons	sugar	3 tablespoons
¾ teaspoon	salt	1 teaspoon
¼ teaspoon	ground nutmeg	½ teaspoon
1¼ teaspoons	bread machine yeast or active dry yeast	1½ teaspoons
⅓ cup	mixed candied fruits and peels	½ cup
	Eggnog Glaze	

Select recipe size. Add all of the ingredients except Eggnog Glaze to a bread machine according to the manufacturer's directions. Select the basic white bread cycle. Drizzle cooled loaf with Eggnog Glaze.

EGGNOG GLAZE: Stir together 1 cup sifted *powdered sugar* and enough *canned or dairy eggnog* (1 to 2 tablespoons) in a small mixing bowl to make a glaze of drizzling consistency.

*NOTE: Our Test Kitchen recommends 1 egg for either size.

**NOTE: For 1½-pound loaf, the bread machine pan must have a capacity of 10 cups or more. For the 2-pound loaf, the bread machine pan must have a capacity of 12 cups or more.

Nutrition facts per slice (¹⁄₁₂): 222 cal., 4 g total fat (1 g sat. fat), 23 mg chol., 170 mg sodium, 42 g carbo., 1 g fiber, 5 g pro. **Daily values:** 3% vit. A, 0% vit. C, 0% calcium, 10% iron

Oatmeal Bread

Try toasting slices of the finished bread for a holiday breakfast, spread with butter and jam, and serve with a big pot of hot tea or hot chocolate.

1½ pound 16 slices	INGREDIENTS	2 pound 22 slices
1 cup	quick-cooking rolled oats	1⅓ cups
⅔ cup	milk	¾ cup
⅓ cup	water	½ cup
1 tablespoon	butter or margarine, cut up	2 tablespoons
2½ cups	bread flour	3⅓ cups
3 tablespoons	packed brown sugar	¼ cup
¾ teaspoon	salt	1 teaspoon
1 teaspoon	bread machine yeast or active dry yeast	1¼ teaspoons

Select recipe size. Spread oats in a shallow baking pan. Bake in a 350° oven for 15 to 20 minutes or until light brown, stirring occasionally. Cool.

Add oats and remaining ingredients to a bread machine according to the manufacturer's directions. If available, select whole grain cycle, or select the basic white bread cycle.

Nutrition facts per slice (¹⁄₁₆): 117 cal., 2 g total fat (1 g sat. fat), 3 mg chol., 115 mg sodium, 22 g carbo., 1 g fiber, 4 g pro. **Daily values:** 1% vit. A, 0% vit. C, 1% calcium, 8% iron

GIVING

What better occasion for sentimental gifts that celebrate family and friendship than the holiday season? To save time, start with ready-made items and embellish them with your own creativity. A sheer curtain can become a tablecloth decorated with pockets for mementoes and snapshots; a purchased photo album becomes a keepsake when you slipcover it with organza. If gift-giving sometimes feels like a duty rather than a pleasure, turn it into an adventure by matching your recipients' interests to a theme. Does your sister-in-law like to relax in a long, hot bath? Give her homemade herbal spa treats. Does your neighbor love to bake chocolate chip cookies? Layer the ingredients in a jar so that all she has to do is add eggs and butter. Gifts with a handmade touch are fun to give and more fun to receive.

from the HEART

Express your affection with sentimental gifts that feature favorite photographs or treasured souvenirs.

pocketful *of* memories

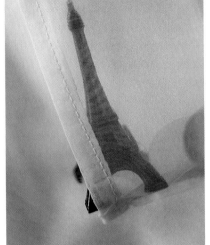

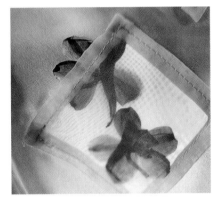

Pocket Tablecloth

This tablecloth makes a wonderful gift for a friend who loves to entertain, or for your own family to enjoy. Insert special photos for holidays or birthdays, pressed flowers for a spring brunch, or dried leaves for an autumn buffet.

here's how...

1 If you're using a curtain, measure and cut it to the desired size, adding 1 inch for hems. Turn under the raw edges, then fold again and topstitch. Use the excess fabric to make the pockets.

2 To estimate how many pockets to make, lay photos of different sizes along one side of the tablecloth. Repeat for the opposite side.

SHOPPING LIST

large organdy or fine linen curtain or 2 sheer tablecloths
thread to match
photos, souvenirs, pressed flowers, herbs, memorabilia

3 Using the photos as patterns, cut pockets from the excess curtain fabric or from the second tablecloth. Add a 1-inch seam allowance all around.

4 Turn under each edge of each pocket twice and press with an iron. Topstitch the top edge of each pocket.

5 Position the pockets on the tablecloth as desired and pin in place. Topstitch around the sides and bottom to secure the pockets to the tablecloth. Press the tablecloth, then tuck photos into the pockets. You also could tuck Christmas cards or small souvenirs into the pockets along with the photos.

Slipcovered Photo Album

SHOPPING LIST

photo album*
1 yard of polyester organza
metallic thread
lightweight fusible adhesive
  tape in ⅝- and ⅞-inch
  widths
photo for the album cover

❧ Turn an ordinary purchased photo album into a keepsake with a silvery slipcover of organza.

Go one step further and make the album an extraordinary gift for a landmark birthday, an anniversary, college graduation, or retirement by filling it with photos of the recipient's family, friends, or activities.

here's how...

1 Measure the album from edge to edge across the spine and add ½ inch. Measure the album from top to bottom and add ½ inch. Cut a rectangle this size from newsprint or newspaper for the album-cover pattern.

2 Cut two pieces of fabric 1 inch larger all around than the pattern.

Center the pattern on the wrong side of one piece of fabric and hold it in place with a book or other weight. Following the manufacturer's instructions, iron the ⅞-inch-wide fusible tape to the fabric along all four sides of the pattern. (This will be the flange that extends beyond the edges of the album.)

4 Remove the pattern. Peel the backing from the fusible tape along the top edge of the slipcover only. Lay the remaining fabric rectangle over the first, wrong sides facing and aligning raw edges. Press to fuse the two fabric rectangles together along the top edge.

To make the pocket for the photo, cut a piece of fabric 1½ inches larger than your photo. Following the manufacturer's instructions, iron a strip of ⅝-inch-wide fusible tape along each edge of the pocket. Position the pocket on the front cover (the right half of the top fabric rectangle). Peel the backing from the fusible tape on three sides of the pocket and iron to adhere the pocket to the cover. Insert the photo, then peel the backing from the remaining edge and iron to adhere.

6 Using metallic thread in both the needle and bobbin, stitch around the photo with a straight stitch.

7 With the front of the slipcover faceup, fold the slipcover in half and press along the fold. Unfold the slipcover and place it with the front (photo side) facedown and cut a slit in the lining between the top and bottom strips of fusible tape. Cut small horizontal slits at

the top and bottom of this slit to equal the width of the album spine. Fold under the raw edges along the slit and fuse them in place with ⅝-inch fusible tape. This gives a neat, finished appearance.

8 Fuse the remaining three edges of the slipcover. Stitch around the inner edge of the fusible tape, using a zig-zag stitch and metallic thread. Trim the raw outer edges even with the outside edge of the fusible tape.

Fold the album covers back and slide the slipcover onto the covers.

*The album shown here is a post-bound album, which can be disassembled to add more pages. The organza slipcover is best for albums with slender spines.

128

11×14-inch wood frame
   with glass and backing
lightweight sandpaper
gold and silver metallic
   acrylic paint
paintbrush
Delta Ceramcoat Fine
   Crackle Finish, Steps 1
   and 2
2 stainless steel cabinet pulls
   4¾ inches long that can
   be screwed to the frame
   from the outside
11×14-inch handmade
   paper, gift wrap, or other
   decorative paper
double-sided adhesive tape
Delta Archival Quality Photo-
   Safe Glue
memorabilia, such as gift
   tags, invitations, photos,
   theatre tickets, etc.
flat ornament, such as a
   crocheted or paper
   snowflake or a brass
   ornament
8 to 12 inches of gold
   ribbon
bits of dried baby's breath
   and maiden-hair fern
crinkled shredded paper
   strips (from a party supply
   store)
4 to 6 spring-type
   clothespins
11×14-inch piece of felt
   (optional)

Christmas Memory Tray

◦⌣ Preserve holiday mementoes inspired by a poem or song in a frame that doubles as a serving tray.

here's how...

1 Carefully remove the backing and glass from the frame.

2 Use sandpaper to roughen the surface of the frame if it's varnished or painted. Wipe off the sanding dust.

3 Paint the frame silver, applying two or more coats if necessary. Smooth the painted surface as needed by rubbing it with a grocery bag or kraft paper.

4 Apply the crackle finish, following the manufacturer's directions.

5 Lightly brush on gold paint, then rub off the excess, leaving gold highlights. Brush gold paint on the silver pulls and rub off for similar highlights on the pulls.

6 Center one pull on each short side of the frame, as shown in the photo, and attach with screws.

7 Secure the handmade paper to the frame backing with double-sided adhesive tape. Arrange memorabilia on top of the paper until you are pleased with the design. To hold large pieces in place, use small pieces of double-sided adhesive tape or dots of glue. Anchor large ribbons in the same manner. Arrange baby's breath and ferns, and scatter shredded paper bits across the design.

8 Place the glass on top and clip the backing and glass together around the edges with the clothespins. This will allow you to hold it all in place as you turn it over to set it in the frame. With the back of the frame facing you, place the piece, glass side down, in the frame, carefully removing one clothespin at a time as you

ease the glass and backing into the frame. Push the pins or brads that came with the frame back in place.

9 If desired, secure a felt rectangle to the back of the frame with double-sided adhesive tape.

Note: Choose a wooden frame with a flat outside edge that is at least ¾ inch wide. When purchasing the pulls, take the frame to the hardware store so you can be sure the pull fits the edge.

Very Personal Gift Tags

here's how...

There's no mistaking who the gift is from when you attach tags like these. Look for sturdy 2×3-inch tags at office supply shops, or cut your own from construction paper. For the photo, write a message in large letters on a piece of construction paper: "From Me," "Happy Holidays," or "Love, Grandma and Grandad." Take a picture of the gift giver holding the paper. A head and chest shot works best. After you have the film developed, take the print to a Kodak copier (they're usually in the film department of a drug store or discount store) and follow the instructions to make nine wallet-size copies. The copier reduces your original image to this size and makes multiple images all at the same time. One sheet costs about $7. If you need more tags, make color photocopies at a copy center for $1 each. Cut away the background, and use a glue stick to attach the photo image to the gift tag.

Other options

The stamp-size photos that accompany a full set of portrait photos from some photo studios are perfect for gift tags. Simply cut them out and glue them onto construction paper. Another option is the sticker film from Polaroid. Look for the cameras and film at discount stores and drug stores. Each photo comes out as a small sticker that you can apply directly to the gift tag.

In a Twinkling:
Gifts

◀ College Survival Kit ($32 or less)

Send your favorite college student back to school armed with plenty of the little necessities: scissors, adhesive tape, office supplies, and a tool kit. First aid supplies also come in handy. Arrange everything in a small plastic wastebasket and decorate it with your student's school pennant and stickers.

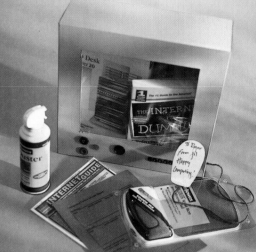

▲ Computer Crazy ($51)

Encourage a novice computer user with accessories such as an ergonomically designed mouse pad, an Internet guidebook, an expandable file for holding software manuals, and canned air for keeping equipment clean. For packaging, cut out the center of the lid of a square gift box. Tape clear cellophane inside and glue buttons to the lower edge. Cut a mouse shape from construction paper for the gift tag.

◀ Kids' Crafts Kit ($16)

Nurture creativity for a niece, nephew, or neighbor's child with this inviting collection of supplies. Shop a discount store for art and crafts supplies. Add scraps of ribbon, yarn, fabric, and other snippets from your own crafting projects. Place everything in a sealable plastic bin, so the packaging doubles as storage.

▼ Office Madness ($19)

Bring some levity to the workplace with this gift for a coworker. Include a Gumby figure for flexibility; a yo-yo for those up-and-down days; marbles, for the days when you've lost yours; bubbles, for when you're bubbling with enthusiasm; a small Etch-a-Sketch for when a picture is worth a thousand words; a Slinky for when you need to spring into action; a matchbox car, for racing from project to project; and adhesive bandages, for patching damaged egos. Pack everything in a small plastic toolbox decorated to look like a first aid kit.

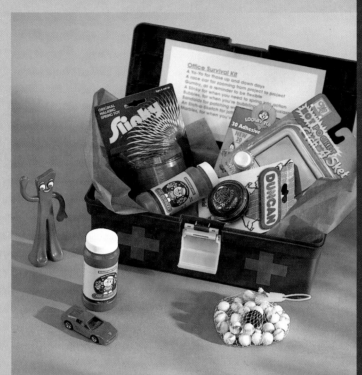

▲ Card Party Pack ($20)

Give the game-playing family on your list a Card Party Pack. Gather a pack of cards, dice, dominoes, scorecards, and a small book of card games. Package them cleverly in a gift box painted red, with playing cards glued around the sides and to the top. Glue a row of dice to the top for a handle.

gifts that give

An increasingly popular alternative to giving "stuff" to family members, neighbors, and friends is to make a donation to a charity in honor of that person. Choose a charity that you know your loved one supports or one that matches his or her interests. Hometown possibilities include a donation to the church building fund, the city botanical gardens, the local food pantry, or in-town toy drive. For international projects, you might start with Heifer Project International (www.heifer.org or 800/422-0474), UNICEF (www.unicef.org or 800/FOR-KIDS), or Alternative Gifts International (www.altgifts.org or 800/842-2243).

Make up a certificate, using a computer or calligraphy, with wording such as "To wish you a happy holiday, a gift has been given in your honor to (fill in the charity's name) by (sign your name)." Attach a brochure about the organization or a short description of its activities. Be creative with packaging. For example, for a gift to the city's botanical gardens, fold the certificate so it fits an empty seed packet. For a donation to the local art museum, slip a postcard of a famous painting into an inexpensive frame and wrap it with the certificate. If your gift to Alternative Gifts International supplies clean drinking water in Kenya, wrap information about the project around a bottle of spring water and present it in a gift bag.

133

Pamper your friends with the luxury of a spa retreat at home.

spa *gifts*

Long soaks in warm, herb-infused waters can relax tense muscles and relieve stress. So treat the people on your gift list to the pleasures of fragrant herbal bath products with bath tea bags, herbal hair rinse, and green-tea body wash. Make the oversize tea bags from interfacing and fill them with herbs to steep in the bathwater. For your friends who prefer showers, mix green tea with unscented body wash for an invigorating cleanser. An herbal hair rinse to use after shampoo leaves hair smelling fresh and fragrant.

Present this at-home spa in a wire basket with a few washcloths or a big fluffy bath towel. Tuck in the hair rinse, tea bags, and body wash, and stitch a bath glove from a pair of washcloths to complete the gift.

bath tea bag

HERBAL MIXES: Shop for dried herbs at health-food stores, or see page 158 for mail-order sources. Don't use crushed herbs intended for cooking; they'll leak out of the tea bag material.
STIMULATING: equal amounts of rosemary leaves, marjoram leaves, peppermint leaves, lavender flowers, and chamomile flowers
RELAXING: equal amounts of lavender flowers, basil, thyme, sage leaves, and rosemary leaves
Add a small amount of oatmeal to each mixture for its skin-softening effects.

SHOPPING LIST
1 yard of 22-inch-wide medium-weight nonwoven interfacing (not fusible-adhesive material)
cotton string
paper tags (from an office supply shop, or make your own from heavy paper)
herbs (see instructions)
oatmeal (optional)
double-sided adhesive tape

here's how...

1 For each bag, cut a 10×16½-inch piece of interfacing. Stitch the long edges together, using a ¼-inch seam. Press the tube so that the seam falls in the center of one side (this will be the wrong side). Press the seam allowances to one side.

2 To make the bottom pleat, fold the tube in half, right sides facing, and press; fold each half again 1 inch away from the center fold, creasing in the opposite direction so the open ends of the tube meet. (The seam will now be on the inside.) Using a paper funnel, fill each side of the bag with about ¼ cup of the desired herb mixture.

3 Align the edges at each end of the tube and fold the corners to the center, making a point. Fold the points down, then fold one point over the other. Staple a loop of string over the folded points.

4 Staple a paper tag to the top of the loop and attach a piece of double-sided adhesive tape to the back of the tag. (Don't remove the backing on the side of the tape facing you.) On the tag, write the ingredients in the herbal mix and include instructions for using the tea bag: Hang the bag over the faucet by the loop. If necessary to keep the tea bag in place while water runs through it, peel off the back of the double-sided tape and press it to the faucet. After bathing, rub the tea bag over your skin for extra soothing benefits.

SHOPPING LIST
loose green tea
unscented body wash (such as Neutrogena Rainbath)

green tea body wash

here's how...

1 Brew one 8-ounce cup of green tea, letting it steep until it is full strength. Pour the tea and leaves into a blender and blend well. Pour the mixture through a sieve to strain out most of the leaves.

2 Add the mixture to the body wash by teaspoonfuls until you like the color.

herbal hair rinse

here's how...

1 Bring 4 cups of distilled water to a boil, then add the desired mixture of herbs and allow to steep for 20 minutes.

2 Strain the mixture into a decorative, shatterproof bottle. Keep refrigerated and use within one week.

bath mitt

here's how...

1 To make a pattern, trace around your hand and wrist on the scrap paper, spreading your fingers slightly. Add ¼ to ½ inch all around the hand and add at least 1 inch on each side of the wrist. Cut out the pattern.

2 Place the pattern on one washcloth, positioning it so the wrist edge falls at the cloth's trimmed edge. Trace around the pattern with a water-soluble marker. Repeat for the remaining washcloth.

3 Cut two pieces of elastic ½ inch shorter than the wrist width. Stitch one piece of elastic to each washcloth at the wrist (in the cloth's trim area). The elastic

should extend ¼ inch beyond the traced wrist lines.

4 From the bias tape, cut an 8-inch length. Stitch the long open edges together, then fold to make a loop.

5 Pin the washcloths together with the elastic aligned and facing out. Sandwich the bias-tape loop between the cloths, with the raw edges at the seam. Stitch around the traced lines, being sure to catch the bias tape loop.

6

Cut out the glove ½ inch beyond the stitching line. Zigzag stitch around the cut edges. Turn the glove inside out. Add a felt leaf at the wrist, if desired.

How can dreams help but be sweet when bed linens are suffused with the fragrance of lavender?

lavender dreams

Everyone appreciates the gift of a good night's sleep. According to traditional Asian medicine, buckwheat-hull pillows help promote rest. The pillow conforms to your head and neck, supporting them comfortably and relieving neck pain and stress. Add lavender buds to encourage relaxation; stitch up a pillowcase to coordinate with the recipient's bedroom colors. For a lighter fragrance, mix up a lavender spray for linens—the pleasure of laying your head on a crisply pressed pillowcase is worth the extra minute or two it takes to spritz and iron the case.

lavender pillow

here's how...

1

If your pillow has a zipper closure, simply unzip and add the cup of lavender flowers. If it doesn't have a zipper, carefully clip the stitches in one seam for about 2 inches. Add the lavender, using a paper funnel, then restitch the opening closed with small blind stitches.

2 Use the plain pillowcase that comes with the pillow for your pattern. Cut one piece of fabric twice the width of the case, adding ½ inch for seam allowances.

3 Encase one long edge of the fabric in the edging lace and stitch; pin the ribbon over the edging on the right side of the case, and stitch close to each edge of the ribbon.

4 Fold the case in half, right sides facing and aligning the raw edges. Stitch the bottom and side seams. Zigzag stitch over the raw edges, then turn the case to the right side and press.

lavender laundry spritz

here's how...

To make the lavender laundry spray, mix 4 ounces of alcohol-based lavender-scented toilet water or room freshener with 24 ounces of distilled water. (Don't use oil-based room sprays as the oil may damage fabric.) Pour the mixture into a clear spray bottle, and make a label from typing paper. Glue it to the bottle with spray adhesive. Include instructions to use the spray on pillowcases or linens just before pressing.

138

Cookies-in-a-Jar

A gift made by hand travels most quickly to the heart (and in this case, to the stomach too). Whether it's something to munch on, hot soup for a cold winter's night, or delicious, homemade candy, a gift of good taste is always the right present.

gifts *from the* kitchen

Cookies-in-a-Jar

Long after all of the holiday treats have been eaten, this pretty, layered, cookie-mix-in-a-jar holds sweet promise for a leisurely day of winter baking. Next time, vary the mix by substituting ⅔ cup candy-coated milk chocolate pieces or ⅔ cup semisweet and/or white baking pieces for the cherries and raisins.

- ¾ cup all-purpose flour
- ½ teaspoon baking powder
- ⅛ teaspoon baking soda
- ⅛ teaspoon salt
- ½ cup butter-flavored or regular shortening
- ½ cup packed brown sugar
- ⅓ cup dried tart cherries
- ⅓ cup golden raisins
- 1 cup rolled oats
- ¼ cup chopped pecans or walnuts
- ¼ cup flaked coconut

Stir together the flour, baking powder, baking soda, and salt in a small mixing bowl. Using a pastry blender, cut in shortening until pieces are pea size.

Starting with the flour mixture, layer the ingredients in a clean 1-quart glass canning jar in the following order (from bottom to top): flour mixture, brown sugar, cherries, raisins, oats, pecans or walnuts, and coconut.

Cover jar and attach a card with the directions for mixing and baking (see sample in box below).

Nutrition facts per cookie: 108 cal., 6 g total fat (1 g sat. fat), 9 mg chol., 30 mg sodium, 13 g carbo., 0 g fiber, 1 g pro. **Daily values:** 1% vit. A, 0% vit. C, 1% calcium, 3% iron

---

Fruit and Nut Oatmeal Drops
(Mix in this jar will keep for 2 weeks.)

Empty contents of the jar into a large mixing bowl. Stir the mixture until combined, using a wooden spoon. Stir in 1 egg and 1 teaspoon vanilla until mixture is well combined. Drop dough by rounded teaspoon 2 inches apart on an ungreased cookie sheet. Bake in a 375° oven for 8 to 10 minutes or until edges are lightly browned. Transfer cookies to a wire rack; cool. Makes about 24 cookies.

---

two gifts in one

■ Package homemade treats (or purchased gourmet specialties) in collectible containers that can be put to other uses after the holidays. Some ideas:

■ Carefully stack cookies in an ironstone tureen. Place the lid on the tureen, then slip ribbon through the handles and tie in a bow over the lid.

■ Fill a vintage carnival-glass bowl with homemade candy, then wrap the dish in opalescent cellophane and tie with ribbon.

■ Fill antique celery glasses or goblets with fudge or truffles.

■ Shop flea markets and antiques stores for enamelware. Small pots with lids are perfect for snack mix or nuts. Slip a bag of biscotti and specialty coffees into an enamelware coffeepot that can hold flowers after the holidays.

peel for the fruit in the cordial recipe (reserve remaining oranges for another use). Steep mixture for 3 weeks.

BANANA CORDIAL: Peel and thinly slice 1 large ripe *banana*. Steep the mixture for 1 week.

MANGO CORDIAL: Peel, pit, and chop 2 ripe *mangoes*. Steep the mixture for 1 to 2 weeks.

PEAR CORDIAL: Peel, core, and thinly slice 6 medium *pears*. Steep the mixture for 3 weeks.

Nutrition facts per ¼ cup: 148 cal., 0 g total fat (0 g sat. fat), 0 mg chol., 1 mg sodium, 14 g carbo., 0 g fiber, 0 g pro. **Daily values:** 0% vit. A, 0% vit. C, 0% calcium, 0% iron

Berry Cordials
Fruit Cordials

Berry Cordials

- 1 cup vodka or gin
- 1½ cups sugar
- 2 cups fresh berries (may substitute a 12- to 16-ounce package frozen unsweetened berries, such as strawberries, blackberries, boysenberries, or lightly sweetened red raspberries, or pitted, dark sweet cherries or tart red cherries)

Heat vodka and sugar in a small saucepan over low heat, stirring just until sugar is dissolved. Remove from heat. Place warmed liquor mixture into a 2-quart glass jar or ceramic container. Stir in berries and cover. Let stand in a cool dark place for 2 to 4 weeks, swirling once a week. Strain as directed in the Fruit Cordials recipe at left. Or, use liquid and berries as a dessert topping. Makes 1⅔ cups cordial and 1¼ cups berries.

Nutrition facts per ¼ cup cordial: 243 cal., 0 g total fat (0 g sat. fat), 0 mg chol., 1 mg sodium, 41 g carbo., 0 g fiber, 0 g pro. **Daily values:** 0% vit. A, 0% vit. C, 0% calcium, 0% iron

Fruit Cordials

For an easy, elegant gift, pour these beautiful cordials into inexpensive cut-glass bottles or unusual decanters. Embellish them with a handmade gift tag and tiny ornaments or holly sprigs tied around the bottle necks. Each fruit will give your cordial a different soft hue.

- 1½ cups sugar
- 1 cup water
  Desired fruit (see suggestions at right)
- 1 750-ml bottle vodka (3½ cups)

Heat sugar and water in a small saucepan over low heat, stirring until sugar is dissolved. Remove from heat; cool. Pour sugar syrup into a 2-quart glass jar. Add desired fruit and vodka; stir gently. Cover the jar with a tight-fitting lid. Let stand (steep) in a cool dark place for the time suggested for each fruit, swirling every few days to distribute the ingredients.

To strain, set a wire strainer, lined with several thicknesses of 100-percent-cotton cheesecloth, over a large bowl or wide-mouth jar. Pour fruit mixture through. If liquid needs further clarifying, pour through a coffee funnel lined with a paper filter. Transfer the strained liquid to a clean, dry bottle using a funnel. Seal bottle tightly and label with contents so you'll be able to identify the flavor. Store at room temperature. Makes about 5 cups.

ORANGE CORDIAL: Remove a thin layer of peel from 3 *oranges* using a sharp knife or vegetable peeler. Take care to avoid the bitter white part. Use

Tomato Split Pea Soup

For a welcome gift of a cold winter night's supper, package the split peas in a glass jar together with the recipe for Tomato Split Pea Soup in a basket lined with a colorful kitchen towel. Add a pretty ladle for serving the finished soup and a package of Cracker Mix.

- 1 cup dry split yellow or green peas
- 1¼ to 1½ pounds meaty smoked pork hocks or one 1- to 1½-pound meaty ham bone
- 2 14½-ounce cans reduced-sodium chicken broth
- 1 cup chopped celery
- ¾ teaspoon snipped fresh tarragon or ¼ teaspoon dried tarragon, crushed
- ¼ teaspoon pepper
- 1 bay leaf
- ⅓ cup tomato paste
- 1 cup sliced carrot
- ½ cup chopped onion
- 1 cup Cracker Mix (see recipe, at right)

Rinse peas. Combine peas, pork hocks or ham bone, chicken broth, 1 cup *water*, celery, dried tarragon (if using), pepper, and bay leaf in a large saucepan or Dutch oven. Bring to boiling; reduce heat. Cover and simmer for 1¼ hours. Remove pork hocks or ham bone; set aside to cool.

Stir tomato paste, carrot, and onion into saucepan. Return to boiling; reduce heat. Cover and simmer for 20 minutes or until vegetables are tender.

Meanwhile, cut meat off bones; coarsely chop meat, discarding bones. Stir meat and fresh tarragon (if using) into saucepan; heat through. Discard bay leaf. Sprinkle each serving with some of the Cracker Mix. Makes 4 to 6 servings.

Nutrition facts per serving: 364 cal., 9 g total fat (2 g sat. fat), 25 mg chol., 1,267 mg sodium, 48 g carbo., 15 g fiber, 25 g pro. **Daily values:** 84% vit. A, 16% vit. C, 7% calcium, 20% iron

Cracker Mix

This fun, crunchy cracker mix is great as a go-with for hot soup (see Tomato Split Pea Soup at left). Or, spice up the mix to munch with a mug of hot cider or a cold beverage—use 2 teaspoons Worcestershire sauce and ¼ teaspoon bottled hot pepper.

- 1 cup bite-size fish-shaped pretzel or cheese-flavored crackers
- 1 cup oyster crackers
- 1 cup bite-size shredded wheat biscuits
- 1 cup bite-size rich round crackers
- 2 tablespoons cooking oil
- ½ teaspoon Worcestershire sauce
- ¼ teaspoon garlic powder
  Dash bottled hot pepper sauce
- 2 tablespoons grated Parmesan cheese

Combine all crackers in a large bowl. Combine cooking oil, Worcestershire sauce, garlic powder, and bottled hot pepper sauce in a small bowl. Pour over cracker mixture, tossing to coat. Sprinkle cracker mixture with Parmesan cheese; toss to coat. Spread mixture in a shallow baking pan.

Bake in a 300° oven for 10 to 15 minutes or until golden, stirring once. Cool completely. Store in an airtight container. Makes 4 cups.

Nutrition facts per ¼ cup: 77 cal., 4 g total fat (0 g sat. fat), 1 mg chol., 113 mg sodium, 10 g carbo., 1 g fiber, 2 g pro. **Daily values:** 0% vit. A, 0% vit. C, 1% calcium, 3% iron

141

Cracker Mix

Cashew-White Fudge Bites

A festive way to package these sweet somethings is to wrap them in clear plastic wrap, then carefully overwrap in foil paper to avoid squashing the cashew toppers.

2 cups sugar
1 5-ounce can (⅔ cup) evaporated milk
½ cup butter
1 6-ounce package white chocolate baking squares, chopped, or one 6-ounce package white baking bars, chopped
½ of a 7-ounce jar marshmallow creme
½ cup chopped cashews
½ teaspoon vanilla
   Cashew halves (optional)

142

Line an 8×8×2-inch baking pan with foil, extending foil over edges of pan. Butter foil; set pan aside.

Butter the sides of a heavy 2-quart saucepan. Combine sugar, evaporated milk, and butter in the saucepan. Cook and stir over medium-high heat until mixture boils. Clip a candy thermometer to side of pan. Be sure the bulb is well covered and not touching bottom of pan. Reduce heat to medium; continue cooking and stirring until temperature registers 236° (7 to 10 minutes). Mixture should boil gently over entire surface.

Remove saucepan from heat; remove thermometer. Add chopped white chocolate; stir until melted. Stir in marshmallow creme, chopped cashews, and vanilla until mixture is combined. Beat by hand for 1 minute.

Pour into prepared pan. Allow fudge to cool and become somewhat firm on the surface (10 to 20 minutes).

Score into four large squares. When candy is firm, use foil to lift it out of pan. Use a knife with a long blade to cut each large square into 4 smaller squares. Then cut diagonally to make a total of 8 triangles for each large square. Repeat with remaining large squares. Lightly press a cashew half into each piece, if desired. Store tightly covered. Makes about 1¾ pounds (32 pieces).

Nutrition facts per piece: 132 cal., 6 g total fat (3 g sat. fat), 10 mg chol., 57 mg sodium, 19 g carbo., 0 g fiber, 1 g pro. **Daily values:** 3% vit. A, 0% vit. C, 2% calcium, 1% iron

Jamaican Jerk Seasoning Mix

Give this versatile spice mix in a small, decorated jar and attach a tag indicating possible uses.

¼ cup sugar
3 tablespoons onion powder
3 tablespoons dried thyme, crushed
2 tablespoons ground allspice
2 tablespoons ground black pepper
3 to 4 teaspoons ground red pepper
1 tablespoon salt
1½ teaspoons ground nutmeg

Combine all ingredients and store in an airtight container. To make ahead, store at room temperature up to 6 months. Makes about 48 teaspoons seasoning mix.

Use to sprinkle or rub over chicken, seafood, meats, or vegetables for grilling or broiling. Or, use the seasoning to spice up simple bean and rice dishes.

Nutrition facts per teaspoon: 8 cal., 0 g total fat (0 g sat. fat), 0 mg chol., 134 mg sodium, 2 g carbo., 0 g fiber, 0 g pro. **Daily values:** 0% vit. A, 0% vit. C, 0% calcium, 1% iron

Cashew-White Fudge Bites

Pear-Berry Gingerbread Loaves

Wrap these diminutive gingerbread loaves in plastic wrap and tie with a yarn bow embellished with small decorative fruits and berries.

    3   cups all-purpose flour
    2   teaspoons baking powder
 1 ½   teaspoons ground cinnamon
    ½   teaspoon baking soda
    ½   teaspoon salt
    2   beaten eggs
    ⅔   cup light-flavored molasses
    ⅔   cup cooking oil
    ½   cup packed brown sugar
    ⅓   cup milk
 1 ½   teaspoons grated gingerroot
    2   medium pears, peeled, cored,
        and finely chopped
        (about 1 cup)
    ½   cup dried cranberries
        Pear Icing

Grease bottoms and halfway up sides of four 5¾×3×2-inch individual loaf pans or eight 4-inch individual fluted tube pans*; set aside.

Combine flour, baking powder, cinnamon, baking soda, and salt in a large mixing bowl. Make a well in the center of flour mixture; set aside. Stir together eggs, molasses, oil, brown sugar, milk, and grated gingerroot in a medium mixing bowl. Add egg mixture all at once to the flour mixture. Stir just until moistened. Fold pears and dried cranberries into batter. Spoon batter into prepared pans.

Bake in a 350° oven for 35 to 40 minutes for loaf pans or about 25 minutes for fluted tube pans, or until a wooden toothpick inserted near the center comes out clean. Cool in pans on wire racks 10 minutes. Loosen and remove from pans. Cool completely on wire racks. Drizzle with Pear Icing. Makes 4 or 8 loaves (16 servings).

PEAR ICING: Stir together 1¼ cups sifted *powdered sugar*, 2 tablespoons *pear liqueur or pear nectar*, and ½ teaspoon *vanilla* in a small mixing bowl. If necessary, stir in a few drops of *milk* to make an icing that is easy to drizzle.
*If your set of fluted tube pans includes only six, chill the remaining batter while the first batch bakes.

Nutrition facts per serving: 291 cal., 10 g total fat (2 g sat. fat), 27 mg chol., 168 mg sodium, 47 g carbo., 1 g fiber, 3 g pro. **Daily values:** 1% vit. A, 1% vit. C, 7% calcium, 13% iron

---

Hot and Spicy Nuts

Package these easy-to-make (and easy-to-eat) nuts for gift-giving in a jar. Tie on a chili pepper decoration and label with a personalized stick-on label.

    1   teaspoon ground coriander
    1   teaspoon ground cumin
    ½   teaspoon salt
    ¼   teaspoon black pepper
    ⅛   teaspoon ground red pepper
    2   cups raw peanuts (or raw
        cashews, almonds, or
        macadamia nuts)
    1   tablespoon cooking oil

Stir together coriander, cumin, salt, black pepper, and red pepper in a small bowl; set aside. Place nuts in a 13×9×2-inch baking pan. Drizzle with cooking oil, stirring to coat. Sprinkle with spice mixture; toss lightly.
Bake in a 300° oven about 20 minutes or until lightly toasted, stirring once or twice. Cool in pan for 15 minutes. Turn out onto paper towels; cool completely. Store, covered, in a cool place. Makes 2 cups.

Nutrition facts per ¼ cup: 225 cal., 20 g total fat (3 g sat. fat), 0 mg chol., 153 mg sodium, 6 g carbo., 3 g fiber, 10 g pro. **Daily values:** 0% vit. A, 0% vit. C, 4% calcium, 9% iron

wishing you a **HOT & SPICY** holiday

from the kitchen of
HEATHER

Hot and Spicy Nuts

143

Turn family photos into gift wrap for small packages. Arrange the color snapshots on a piece of 11×17-inch white paper and tack them in place with loops of adhesive tape. Copy the collage on a color copier as many times as desired for gift wrap. (Remember to choose the 11×17-inch paper tray when you begin copying.)

In a Twinkling:
Gift Wraps

Wrapped packages that have to be shipped don't have to be boring just because they shouldn't have bows. Use a decorative paper from an art supply store to wrap the box. Then wrap two lengths of ribbon around the box, leaving enough room for a second, wider ribbon to be centered between them. Glue the ribbons to the box, then layer a third kind of ribbon over these.

Here's a gift that comes complete with treats. Wrap the box with bright red paper, then glue layers of ribbon in graduated sizes around the center of the box. Use thick white crafts glue or hot glue to attach wrapped peppermint candies to the box top. (If you use shiny paper, glue the candies with crafts glue rather than hot glue.)

◀ Present a small package in a botanical print. Make a color copy of a print (be sure to use noncopyrighted images), and wrap the box. For larger boxes, enlarge the image on the copier as needed.

▲ Use a hot-glue gun to attach vintage buttons (or other buttons collected from flea markets and garage sales) to the top of a package in a tree shape. Ivory-color vintage buttons on natural or brown wrapping paper make a stylish yet romantic combination; for a more colorful effect, combine jeweled buttons on a colored paper. To remove the buttons from the paper, place the discarded gift wrap in a plastic freezer bag in the freezer; the buttons will pop off.

▲ Wrap a square box with parchment paper, then use 1½-inch-wide velvet ribbon to tie a 6-inch-diameter vine wreath to the top. Glue one end of a piece of ribbon around the wreath, pull the ribbon taut around the box, and glue the remaining end around the wreath. Repeat for the second ribbon. Glue velvet millinery leaves to the wreath, if desired.

KIDS'

'Tis the season to be crafting, and a day of making gifts and ornaments is a great way to get in the holiday spirit. The crafts on the following pages are fun for kids to make themselves (with a little adult help) or for adults to make for the children on their gift lists. Preteens can make the bath mitt on pages 152–53, and it's a great opportunity for them to pick up some basic needlework skills they may not learn anywhere else. Even kindergarten-age children can help paint bowls and pillowcases for pet gifts—or use the same paint pens to decorate cereal or soup bowls for each member of the family. Teens with a creative bent also may enjoy making the stamped floor rug and window scarf on pages 12 and 13 for their own rooms. It's never too early to nurture the artist within.

STUFF

good-quality (at least 200-count) plain white cotton pillowcase
cardboard or heavy kraft paper to fit inside the pillowcase
low-tack painter's tape
permanent fabric markers (pigment fabric dye markers with a brush or felt tip work the best)
large paw print stamp (see page 158 for a mail-order source)
fabric ink stamp pads (see page 158 for a mail-order source)
iron
self-adhesive hook-and-loop tape to fit the open end of the pillowcase (20 inches for most standard cases)
zippered cotton pillow protector with the tightest weave available
1 to 2 cu. feet shaved cedar bedding chips (available at pet stores)

crafts *for kids*

Remember the furry, four-legged members of your family with these gifts. All of these projects are easy enough for kids to make with just a little help from an adult.

design ideas

ALL PETS: pet names, nicknames, paw prints, geometric designs, such as lines, zig zags, squiggles, swirls, spirals, dots
CATS: "I love my cat," fish, mice, pictures of your cat, "here, kitty, kitty," "good cat," and other cat phrases
DOGS: "I love my dog," bones, pictures of your dog, "good dog," "arf," "woof," "bow-wow," obedience commands like "come, sit, stay," and other dog phrases

Personalized Pet Pillow

here's how...

1 Wash and dry the pillowcase; do not use fabric softener or detergent with additives. Iron the pillowcase, then slip the cardboard or kraft paper inside to keep the paints from bleeding through. Tape the pillowcase to your work surface so the fabric is smooth but not distorted.

2 Paint your designs with the fabric markers. Add stamped paw prints to fill in empty spaces. After the paint and ink are dry, heat-set them by ironing over them with a dry iron set to the cotton setting.

3 Place the hook-and-loop tape along the opening of the pillowcase with the stiff hook side to the top side of the opening and the soft loop side to the bottom of the opening.

4 Fill the pillow protector with cedar bedding chips. (The amount will vary with the size of your pet and how much "give" you want the pillow to have.) Place the liner in the pillowcase and seal the edges shut with the hook-and-loop tape.

Personalized Pet Dishes

here's how...

1 Wash the bowls with warm soapy water, then rinse and dry thoroughly.

2 Shake the markers well, then pump the tip to start the paint flowing. Paint designs on the outside of each bowl. (If you make a mistake or want to redo part of the design, remove the paint with a cotton swab. If the paint has dried, first dip—but do not saturate—the swab in rubbing alcohol.) Let the bowl(s) dry for 24 hours.

3 Place the bowl(s) in a cold oven; keep the oven door open slightly. Heat the oven to 300°. Note: You may smell a slight chemical odor. When the oven reaches 300°, close the door and bake the bowl(s) for 35 minutes. Turn off the oven, open the door slightly, and allow the bowl(s) to cool completely. The paint is now dishwasher-safe.

***Note:** The Porcelaine felt-tipped paint pens are made specifically for painting on ceramics and glass and are dishwasher-safe after you bake the items in an ordinary oven. The same paints are available in a bottle or tube, but the markers are easiest for kids to use and are less messy.

149

Catnip Toys

here's how...

1 Turn the bootie heel-side-up. Just above the toe seamline, pinch about ¼ to ⅜ inch to form a nose. Wrap embroidery floss around the base of this pinched area 8 times, then tie it off to form a nose. This also makes the toe seamline curve upward to form a smile. In the same way, make 2 ears in front of the bootie's heel.

2 Lightly stuff the bootie with fiberfill, leaving room in the center of the bootie for a small amount of catnip. Add the catnip, then finish stuffing the bootie.

3 Cut the yarn into three 1-yard lengths. Fold the yarn in half and tie the top of the bootie closed. Using overhand knots, tie the 6 strands of yarn together about every inch. Trim the yarn tails after the final knot.

4 Using the fabric marker, make eyes and outline the smile.

5 For the whiskers, thread 12 inches of embroidery floss onto a blunt-tip needle. Stitch through the snout area to the other side, then back to the first side, taking a very small stitch. The needle should exit the snout just a few threads away from where it entered. Pull the floss tightly and knot it, drawing in the snout to form a narrower nose. Repeat with a second color of floss. Make whiskers on the other side of the face in the same manner. Trim the whiskers as desired.

Crafts Stick Ornaments

 Set aside an afternoon to make these ornaments with your children or grandchildren. They'll make wonderful teachers' gifts or package toppers.

basic directions:
here's how...

An adult should do all cutting, using scissors or pruning shears to cut the crafts sticks. Apply paint to the back and side edges as well as to the front of each stick. For the hanging loop, glue the ends of an 8-inch-long piece of jute or ribbon to the back of the ornament at the top.

nutcracker

1 Use one jumbo and two narrow crafts sticks and a star sticker. Cut one narrow stick in half for the arms. Cut a 1-inch piece from each end of the second narrow stick for the boots.

2 Measure from the top of the jumbo stick and make tiny marks at 1 inch, 2 inches, and 3¾ inches. Paint the sticks as follows: apply flesh-tone paint between the 1-inch and 2-inch marks and to the rounded ends of the arm sticks; apply red paint from the 2-inch mark to the 3¾-inch mark. Paint the remaining sections of the arm sticks red. Paint the remaining areas of the jumbo stick blue. Paint the boots black.

3 Paint the face and uniform details as shown, using yellow, white, and black opaque paint markers. Adhere a star sticker to the hat.

4 Glue the arms to the body, allowing them to extend beyond the body about ¼ inch. Glue the boots to the bottom of the body, allowing the ends to extend slightly beyond the bottom of the body stick.

reindeer

1 Use one jumbo crafts stick. You'll also need a small piece of brown crafts foam, ⁵⁄₁₆-inch beady eyes, black dimensional paint, one red mini pompom, a small jingle bell, and narrow red ribbon.

2 Cut the jumbo stick in half so it's about 3 inches long. Paint the stick brown.

3 Transfer the antler pattern *at right* to the crafts foam and cut two. Glue the antlers to the back of the head.

4 Glue the beady eyes about 1 inch from the top. Use black dimensional paint to draw the nose and mouth line, then glue the red pompom as shown. Glue the hanger to the back of the head. Tie the small jingle bell to the hanger with ribbon.

penguin

1 Use one jumbo and one narrow crafts stick; you'll also need orange crafts foam, ³⁄₁₆-inch beady eyes, narrow ribbon, and felt.

2 Paint the jumbo stick white and let it dry. Cut 1½ inches from each end of the narrow stick for the wings (discard the rest). Paint the wings black. Also paint a

narrow line of black along the edges of the white jumbo stick.

3 Transfer the beak and feet patterns below to orange crafts foam and cut them out. Glue the beady eyes, beak, and feet to the body. Glue the wings to the back of the stick, about 2 inches from the top of the head.

4 To make the hat, cut a 1×4-inch strip of felt. Fold it in half and tie a narrow ribbon ½ inch from the fold to gather the top of the hat. Clip the fold, then cut the felt to fringe it. Glue the penguin's head inside the open ends of the hat. Cut a long, narrow strip of matching felt for the scarf. Fringe the ends and glue it in place.

151

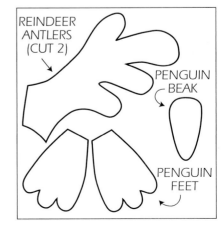

REINDEER ANTLERS (CUT 2)

PENGUIN BEAK

PENGUIN FEET

Bath Time Treats

Adults may view bath time as an opportunity to relax, but for kids, it's usually a chore. To make bath time fun, give kids their own "spa gifts," in the form of bath mitts and holiday-shaped soaps. The mitts are good projects for beginning sewers and great gifts for younger siblings or cousins. To use the mitt, slip a bar of soap in the bottom pocket; the child's hand goes in the middle or top pocket.

152

bath mitts

here's how...

1 Fold the washcloth in half. Whipstitch the long edges together from corner to corner, leaving both ends open.

2 Refold the cloth so the stitched area runs down the middle and the folded edges are at the sides.

3 Fold the cloth in half with the stitched edges lined up on the inside. Pin the sides together through the folds.

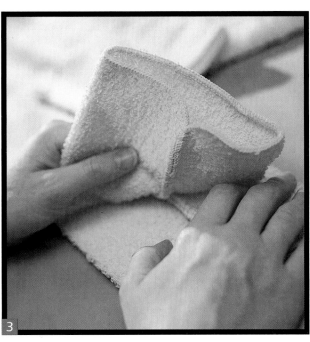

4 Stitch the pinned sides, using small whip stitches.

5 If desired, use contrasting embroidery floss to blanket stitch around the three closed edges, leaving the top edges open.

6 To stitch a monogram or an animal face, use embroidery floss and stitch through one outside layer only. Use a back stitch to outline ears in the corners and to draw in the mouth; use satin stitch for the nose and tongue and French knots for the muzzle. For the eyes, make four straight stitches in an asterisk shape. Knot threads on the inside.

Dreft or Ivory Snow baby
   detergent
water
food coloring
cookie cutters
paintbrush
liquid hand soap or lotion
glitter

holiday soaps

here's how...

1 In a mixing bowl, combine two cups of baby detergent, several drops of food coloring, and ¼ cup of water. Mix well, and continue adding small amounts of water until the mixture is the consistency of cookie dough. (The amount of water will vary according to geographic location and humidity.)

2 To make a marbled dough, knead two different colors of dough together.

3 Sprinkle some detergent onto a flat work surface (as if you were flouring a surface to knead bread dough). Roll out the dough or press it with your hands until it's about ½ inch thick.

4 Using the cookie cutters, cut out shapes from the soap dough. Push the soap out of the cutters carefully; the damp dough is fragile and can break. Set the soap shapes aside and let them air-dry.

5 Mix liquid hand soap or lotion with glitter and use it to paint the soaps for a shiny finish.

153

Family Game

Playing board games is a great way to nurture togetherness, and this game should keep everyone talking. Use your own family's history to make up the questions and have every family member help. When everyone gathers for the holidays, bring out the game and enjoy an afternoon of laughter, sharing memories, and passing along family stories to the next generation.

here's how...

1 With a pencil, draw a heart shape on the drawing paper, nearly filling the paper. Erase the line in the upper left hand section to make the starting point of the game. Lightly draw a pair of spiral lines from the starting point to the center, creating a path that's at least 1½ inches wide. At the center, mark the end of the path with a small heart.

2 Divide the path into spaces no smaller than 1 inch. Draw over all pencil lines with the broad-tip marker. With the fine-tip marker, write on random spaces a variety of game actions such as "Lose 1 turn" or "Jump ahead 3 spaces." Other ideas for game actions include: Blow a kiss to each player, hug each player, give the player on your right a high-five, trade places with another player, dance a jig, take an extra turn, or sing a song.

3 Print "Draw 1 card" on eight or more spaces along the path.

4 Print your family's name at the center of the heart shape.

5 With the crayons or colored pencils, color the center heart red; color all "Draw 1 card" spaces turquoise; color all spaces with game actions orange. Randomly color the remaining spaces with four to six other colors of your choice. Each color will represent a topic for the game. You may want to leave two or three colors as free spots without a topic. For durability, use rubber cement to attach the paper to a piece of foam-core board, then cover it with clear self-adhesive shelf liner.

6 Make up four to six topics and assign each one a color (see the Topics Key for ideas). Write this key on the game board or on a separate piece of paper.

7 For the game cards, draw a heart on the back of each 3×5 note card. Before you begin to play, give each player several note cards and ask him or her to write down something about a family member on each card but not to write that person's name. (For example, "This person was in World War II," "This person won a prize at a horse show," "This person broke a leg," "This person plays the violin.") Stack the cards facedown near the game board.

To play, each person chooses a game piece and places it at the starting point. Players take turns flipping the coin. Heads means move the game piece ahead one space; tails means move ahead two spaces. The youngest person goes first. When you land on a colored space, do what the Topics Key tells you. When you land on a turquoise space, draw the top card, read it out loud, and try to guess whom it describes. If you guess correctly, you stay where you are; if you guess incorrectly, you lose your next turn. The first person to reach the heart of the family wins.

154

These 2 pe
look school t
Washington D

topics key

■ Yellow: player must
tell about something
that makes him happy

■ Pink: player must tell
about something for
which she is thankful

■ Green: player must
tell something funny

■ Purple: player must
share a long-ago
memory

■ Orange: player
must do whatever the
space indicates

■ Turquoise: player
must draw a card

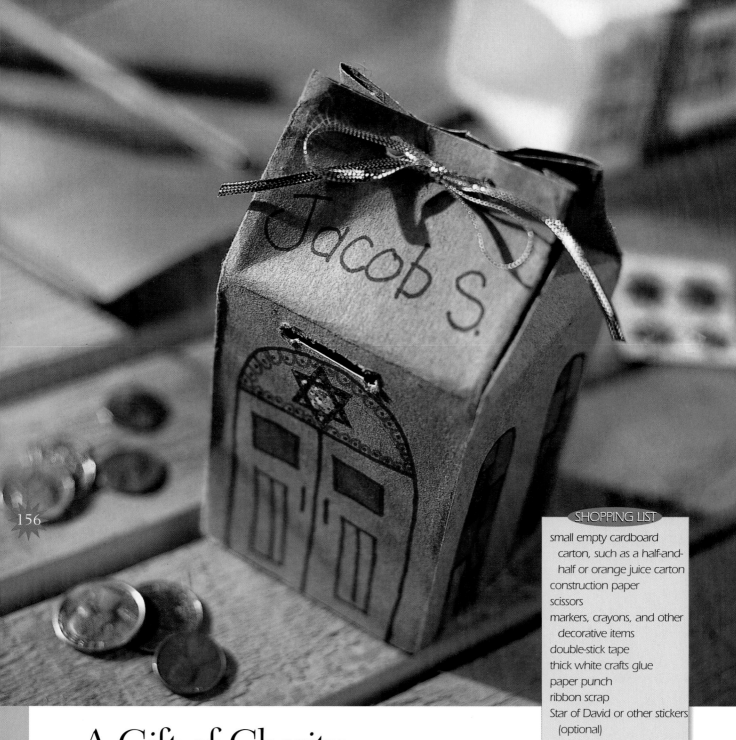

A Gift of Charity

The Hebrew word for charity is *tzedakah*, and the tzedakah box is one that Jewish children pass around in class or keep at home to add contributions throughout the year. When the box is full, the children usually help choose the charity to which the money goes. These boxes are easy for children to make and are appropriate for exchanging with friends as Hanukkah gifts.

here's how...

1 Carefully open out the carton top and wash and dry it thoroughly.

2 Cut construction paper to fit around the carton, allowing for a slight overlap at the beginning and end. Wrap the paper around the carton and mark the corners, then remove the paper and fold it along these lines.

3 Using markers or crayons, decorate the paper to resemble a temple, home, or other building. Tape and glue the paper around the carton. Cut a slit in one side for inserting coins.

4 Fold the carton top closed and punch two holes through the top flange. Run ribbon through the holes and tie the carton closed. Add stickers or other decorations.

Autographed Overnight Bag

Start with a plain pillowcase to make a carryall for slumber parties.

Fabric paints take the place of a buttonhole attachment to edge the buttonholes on this bag. Give a laundry marker or fabric marker with the bag, so the recipient can collect her friends' autographs at each party.

here's how...

1 Place the pillowcase on a flat surface. Mark the center of the hemmed edge. Make another mark 2 inches on each side of the center. Position the plastic lid between the marks and trace around the lower half. Cut along the line through all layers of fabric. This will be the opening for the handle.

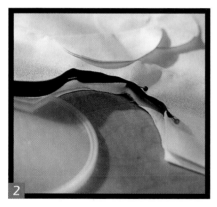

Separate the curved cut edges. Bind each edge with double-fold bias tape. Use a running stitch through all layers close to the outer edges of the binding.

3 Sew a button at the center of one side near the stitching on the hem. Sew an additional button 1½ inches in from each side of the pillowcase.

4 Fold the bottom of the pillowcase toward the hem with the side edges even. The pillowcase bottom should extend at least ½ inch beyond the top of the buttons. With chalk, mark the center top of each button on the pillowcase

plain pillowcase in a pastel color
plastic 4-inch margarine lid
scrap of cardboard
From a fabric store:
    thread to match pillowcase
    double-fold bias tape
    3 large buttons
    dressmaker's chalk
From a crafts store:
    dimensional paints
    acrylic crafts paint in the
        desired color
    clear acrylic spray, laundry
        markers, or colored fabric
        markers (optional)
From a hardware store or
    crafts store:
    ¼ inch diameter wooden
        dowel cut into two 16-
        inch pieces (lumber-
        supply companies will
        make the cuts for you)

bottom. Draw a vertical line where the buttonhole will be. Make the line at least ¼ inch longer than the button's diameter.

Cut the buttonhole openings with a sharp scissors through both layers of fabric. Slip buttons through the holes to check the fit. Cut three strips of cardboard to fit through the buttonholes. Insert a strip through each buttonhole and tip it sideways. Paint along the cut edge of each buttonhole with dimensional paint. Let dry, then paint the remaining cut

edges. Repeat on the opposite side of the pillowcase and use enough paint to make the fabric layers adhere to each other.

 157

Paint the dowels. Let dry. To insert them in the pillowcase, make a small slit at one side near the top edge. Slide the dowels through the slit and into the hems on each side of the opening.

7 To use, put pajamas and other overnight essentials into the open bag. Fold it in half and button it up to carry it. To launder, hand-wash and air-dry.

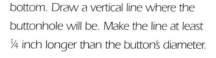

credits & sources

Unless otherwise noted, all styling by Jil Severson and all photos by Peter Krumhardt.

pages 8–13 designs: Jil Severson; assistant stylist: Jenny Stoffel; pillows: Sonja Carmon. Order stamps (Personal Stamp Exchange #E-1272 Hallelujah, #E-1214 Peace, #K-1624 Noel), Fabrico Premium Multi-Purpose Craft Ink stamp pads, reinking liquid, and fabric pens from Outstamping Designs, 215 5th St., West Des Moines, IA 50265; 515/277-5719. Tara floor cloth canvas and 1-inch-wide Economy Artist's Tape available through Dick Blick; call 800/828-4548 to order, request a catalog, or find the nearest store.

pages 14–17 designs and styling: Heidi Kluzak; photos: King Au; how-to styling: Jil Severson; photos: Peter Krumhardt

pages 18–23 design and styling: Peggy Johnston

page 24 top, design and styling: Michele Michael; photo: Jeff McNamara; center, styling: Heidi Kluzak; photo: King Au; bottom, styling: Mauer/Rose

page 25 top, design and styling: Michele Michael; photo: Jeff McNamara; center, styling: Lisa Cicotte; bottom, design and styling: Paula Hamilton; photo: James Yochum

pages 26–27 design: Breaca Lozier and Libby Becker, Special Arrangements

pages 28–29 designs: Nancy Worrell. After February 1, 2001, kits for the curly wire ornament may be ordered from Nancy Worrell's website, http://hometown.aol.com/designsby

pages 30–31 designs: Peggy Johnston

pages 32–35 styling: Heidi Kluzak and Mary Anne Thomson; photos: Steven McDonald; how-to photo: Peter Krumhardt

pages 36–37 designs and styling: Mary Mulcahy and Paula Hamilton; photos: James Yochum

page 38 top, design and styling: Michele Michael; photo: Jeff McNamara; bottom, design and styling: Peggy Johnston

page 39 top, design and styling: Laura Holthorf Collins; photo: King Au; bottom, design: Beth D. Stevens

pages 40–43 mantel and Maccabee pillow concepts: Niki Reese Eschen; mantel styling: Peggy Johnston; pillow design: Barb Vaske; pillow execution: Sonja Carmon

page 44 top left, design and styling: Peggy Johnston; center, Mary Mulcahy and Paula Hamilton; photo: James Yochum; bottom, Jil Severson; photo: Hopkins Associates

page 45 top, design and styling: Michele Michael; photo: Jeff McNamara; bottom left, design and styling: Jil Severson; photo: Hopkins

Associates; bottom right, design and styling: Peggy Johnston

pages 46–47 designs: Jil Severson

pages 48–53 designs: Jim Williams

pages 54–59 designs: Cort Schwanebeck

page 60 top left, design and styling: Nancy Wall Hopkins and Joe Boehm; photo: Michael Skott; top right, design and styling: Libby Becker and Breaca Lozier, Special Arrangements; bottom, design and styling: Mary Mulcahy and Paula Hamilton; photo: James Yochum

page 61 top, design and styling: Heidi Kluzak and Mary Anne Thomson; photo: Steven McDonald; bottom left, design and styling: Libby Becker and Breaca Lozier, Special Arrangements; bottom right, design and styling: Mary Mulcahy and Paula Hamilton; photo: James Yochum

page 63 styling: Michele Michael; photo: Jeff McNamara

pages 64, 66, 69, 70 food stylists: Charles Worthington, Jennifer Peterson

page 72 food stylist: Charles Worthington

page 73 illustrator: Gary Palmer

pages 74, 77–78 food stylist: Dianna Nolin; photo: Mike Dieter

page 80 concept: Niki Reese Eschen; design and styling: Peggy Johnston

pages 82–85 food stylist: Lynn Blanchard; photos: Perry Struse; how-to stylist: Jennifer Peterson; photo: Peter Krumhardt

pages 86–87 design and styling: Nancy Wall Hopkins and Joe Boehm; photo: Michael Skott; how-to styling: Jil Severson; photo: Peter Krumhardt

pages 88–89, 98–99 design and styling: Peggy Johnston

pages 90–91 design: Barb Vaske

pages 92–93, 96 design and styling: Nancy Wall Hopkins and Joe Boehm; photos: Michael Skott

pages 94–95, 97 design and styling: Libby Becker and Breaca Lozier, Special Arrangements

page 100 food stylist: Jennifer Peterson

page 101 food stylist: Janet Pittman; photo: Mike Dieter

page 102 food stylist: Janet Pittman; photo: Andy Lyons

page 104 food stylist: Janet Pittman; photo: Scott Little

page 105 food stylist: Jennifer Peterson; photo: Mike Dieter

page 107 photo: Paula Bronstein/Stone

pages 106, 108 food stylist: Jennifer Peterson

page 109 food stylist: Charles Worthington

page 110 top left, bottom left, design and styling: Nancy Wall Hopkins and Joe Boehm;

photos: Michael Skott; right, design and styling: Libby Becker and Breaca Lozier, Special Arrangements

page 111 right, design and styling: Karen J.M. Tack; photo: Bill Holt; bottom, design and styling: Nancy Wall Hopkins and Joe Boehm; photo: Michael Skott

page 112 food stylist: Charles Worthington

page 115 food stylist: Janet Pittman; photo: Scott Little

pages 116–17 food stylists: Charles Worthington, Jennifer Peterson

page 118 food stylist: Dora Jonassen; photo: Mark Thomas

pages 119–120, 123 food stylist: Jennifer Peterson

pages 126–27 design: Heidi T. King; styling: Jil Severson and Jenny Stoffel

pages 128–29 design, styling: Peggy Johnston

page 130 design: Nancy Worrell; styling: Jil Severson and Jenny Stoffel

page 131 concept: Paula Marshall; design: Jil Severson

pages 132–33 design: Jil Severson

pages 134–37 design, styling: Peggy Johnston. Order herbs and other aromatherapy supplies from Tom Thumb Workshops, 10 Holly St., Onancock, VA; 800/526-6502; or visit their website: www.tomthumbworkshops.com

page 138 food stylist: Jennifer Peterson

pages 140–41 food stylist: Lynn Blanchard; photo: Mike Dieter

page 142 food stylist: Jennifer Peterson

page 143 photo: Andy Lyons

pages 144–45 top left, produced by Michele Michael; photo: Jeff McNamara; remaining photos, designs: Jim Williams; photos: Peter Krumhardt

pages 148–50 design: Jil Severson. Paw print stamp by Fabricated Art, stamp pad available through Outstamping Designs (see under pages 8–13). Porcelaine 150 paint pens and Pebeo paints available at arts and crafts stores nationwide, or check their website: www.pebeo.com

pages 151–53 ornament and bath mitt designs: Beth D. Stevens; soap design: Heidi T. King

pages 154–55 design: Beth D. Stevens

page 156 design: Jil Severson

page 157 design: Beth D. Stevens

index

159

index *continued*

160